A TREASURY OF INSPIRATIONAL READINGS

F E STALLAN

JOHN RITCHIE LTD

CHRISTIAN PUBLICATIONS

Copyright © John Ritchie Ltd. 1997
First published in the UK 1998 by John Ritchie Ltd,
40 Beansburn, Kilmarnock, Scotland KA3 1RH

ISBN: 0 946351 78 3

Scripture quotations are taken from King James Version.

Designed and produced for the publishers by
Gazelle Creative Productions, Concorde House,
Grenville Place, Mill Hill, London NW7 3SA.

CONTENTS

PREFACE

*F*red Stallan was converted in the early 1940's in the city of Glasgow, and from then on gave himself to the study of the Scriptures and to the ministry of the Word of God. Over the years he became widely appreciated and was held in high esteem by the Lord's people for his ministry and his biblical scholarship, preaching at meetings and conferences throughout the British Isles and also further afield.

When he retired from hospital administration in 1986, he took up the position of Secretary of the Lord's Work Trust in Kilmarnock, Scotland. This Trust acts as an avenue for funds being sent to evangelists and missionaries throughout the world, gifts being forwarded to the beneficiaries at the end of each month, accompanied by a letter from the Secretary.

From November 1986, every month for over eleven years, Fred Stallan wrote the Secretary's letter to the Lord's servants. His letters, based on a phrase of Scripture, elicited great appreciation from those who received them. Notes of deep gratitude were received from every quarter of the globe, many telling of special help and encouragement given in often difficult circumstances. Usually he added a personal note in his own beautiful handwriting, and developed a strong friendship over the years with hundreds of the Lord's servants around the world, many of whom he had never met. Altogether he wrote one hundred and thirty-four letters, the last one dated 31st December 1997 – the day before his homecall.

As a tribute to their friend and colleague, and in response to many requests to have these letters preserved in a more permanent form, the Trustees of the Lord's Work Trust have commissioned this book, which is a compilation of his letters over these years. They have been published in this book without alteration to his original text. It is their desire that these letters will be a blessing and encouragement to a wider circle than has been possible until now, and that the Lord will be further glorified through these writings of this very dear brother.

The Trustees
Lord's Work Trust

August 1998

5

ILLUSTRATIONS

CONTRIBUTORS:

Alan Bedding, Gerry Bessent, Roger Chouler, David Ford, Peter Ford,
Glyn Lewis, Sue Hull, Peter Wyart.

*Beloved, I pray that you may prosper in all things and **be in health just as your soul prospers.*** 3 JOHN 1:2

*T*here is a very interesting combination of word and thought in the second verse of John's 3rd Epistle. Written to a man named Gaius, the opening words intimate a prayer on his behalf. It is an all-embracing prayer, possibly reading, 'Beloved, in all respects I pray,' or 'Beloved, I pray that in all things thou mayest prosper.'

It would seem that this man Gaius was in poor health, perhaps even brought on by the burden of testimony-bearing, if the teaching of the Epistle is anything to go by. Whatever the reason, the concern of the writer is clear, health and prosperity for Gaius was his deep exercise. Now there the matter might have rested, in the normal way of life, but John had another thought; something of great moment.

The additional words, 'even as thy soul prospereth,' carry the prayer into another category. Were those words regulatory? Was John praying for the health and prosperity of Gaius only if health and prosperity of soul kept pace? Was the importance of the body's health to be judged by a corresponding prosperity of soul? The contemplation of the thought opens up a very challenging consideration. It is possible that things can get out of balance so that prayer for prosperity of body takes precedence over prayer for prosperity of soul? Is there a spiritual regulator? Is the higher life the real barometer?

The many questions which spring to mind serve to remind us of the profound situation described by a well-known teacher, that prayer is 'the Divine within us crying to the Divine above us,' and yet again the words of E. M. Bounds in his book, *The weapon of prayer* that 'Prayer is the soul of a man stirred to plead with God for men.'

I *press toward the mark* for the prize of the high calling of God in Christ Jesus. PHILIPPIANS 3:14

*T*he first five words of Philippians 3:14, 'I press towards the mark,' although only three words in the original, are variously translated in the many different versions of the Scriptures. The R.V., for example, gives the rendering, 'I press on towards the goal.'

However rendered, one cannot miss the attitude of Paul as he stretched out for the prize, like the athlete in the games, flat out for the tape, with no eye for anything else but the goal. This runner never looked back; he could not, his body was stretched forward in the direction towards which he ran; the goal was his all-absorbing object. Paul had heard the upward call of God and it drew him on. The prize before him was that he might win Christ in the resurrection state. Until he reached that state, his sole concern in the world was to press on towards the mark.

History has many examples of those who pressed on towards a mark, only to be met with disappointment when the goal was reached. Not so in the Christian life; no disappointment there, Christ the Lord is at the end of the journey. Associated with Christopher Columbus there are two significant words. In his historic voyage, his sailors rebelled and begged him to return to Spain as they were lost in that vast ocean. The answer of Columbus to his crew as he pointed west was only two words, 'Sail on!'

And the LORD *spake unto Moses, saying,* **Make thee two trumpets of silver**. NUMBERS 10:1,2

The first words of Numbers Chapter 10 introduce a unique system of communication. For the very vital business of calling an assembly or other important matters, the means specified by God to the Israelites was the trumpets' call. The two trumpets were made of silver and they were to the nation a constant reminder of the cost of redemption. New Testament revelation tells of the real cost of redemption by the word of Peter, 'We were not redeemed with such corruptible things as silver and gold … but with the precious blood of Christ.' To which may be added a word by Paul, 'Ye are not your own, for ye are bought with a price: therefore glorify God in your body, and in your spirit, which are God's.'

Two of the trumpet calls were different from the others and were called alarms. The first of the alarm calls was a direction to break camp and move forward. It was not an uncertain sound; it was a clarion call from God that there was to be no settling down, no permanency in the wilderness; the promised land was on before. When the camp was struck, the cloud moved and the people of Israel, with standards raised, and with royal Judah in the front, journeyed forward.

At the commencement of another year, it is good to be reminded that here we have no continuing city. The call of God is clear that our citizenship is in heaven from whence also we look for the Saviour. What then shall be our attitude as we move forward into a new year? Perhaps the words of Carrie Breck's hymn have a voice for us:

Lifetime is working time, do thy honest part,
Though in discouragement, bear a cheerful heart,
Trusting Jesus as thy friend, ne'er from Him depart,
Work, ever work for Jesus.

*But I would ye should understand, brethren, that the things which happened unto me have fallen our rather unto **the furtherance of the gospel**...* PHILIPPIANS 1:12

When Paul wrote to the Philippians he used a very telling word at the beginning of the Epistle to describe the progress of the Gospel. Circumstances which were not congenial to him personally were not reckoned to be of much consequence; what he had before him was the steady advance of the message of glad tidings. His choice of word to describe the advance takes into account that the way forward may not be easy but that the message in itself had an uncanny power for cutting through opposition. Some have used the word 'furtherance' to describe the progress of the pioneer cutting a way through thick undergrowth; not easy, but steadily forward. This gives confidence to the bearers of the good news, that despite difficult conditions, the Gospel will cut its own path as it onward goes.

Although the noun form of the word in Philippians 1:12 is vibrant with meaning, the verb form of the word is not without its message of encouragement. Luke uses it in connection with our Lord, 'And Jesus **increased** in wisdom and stature, and in favour with God and man.' In Nazareth, as a boy, as a youth and as a man at His trade, His advance in the neighbourhood was noted. Perhaps there was some opposition; it is hard to imagine that He would be free of it, even in His early days. Whatever the circumstances, Jesus advanced steadily and with perfect balance of life before God and man.

The Sankey hymn catches a little of the challenge of going forward:

> *In this little moment then, Onward Go!*
> *In thy ways acknowledge Him; On-ward Go!*
> *Let His mind be found in thee;*
> *Let His will thy pleasure be;*
> *Thus in life and liberty, On-ward Go!*

*T*here are many weighty expressions in the Authorised Version of the Scriptures. Not least amongst them are the words of command to Abram in Genesis 12:1, 'Abram get…out!' Or the words of command to Joshua in Joshua 1:2, 'Joshua…go over!' Abram went out, and Joshua went over. One set out on the pathway of faith and the other commenced the occupation of the promised land on the other side of Jordan.

In the New Testament, Colossians 4:17 records words of command to the Colossians, 'And say to Archippus, take heed!' Now, to what was he to take heed? It was the ministry he had received from the Lord. The question then arises, 'Did he take heed?' The answer may well depend on whether Colossians was written before Philemon. If so, then it would seem that Archippus did take heed, because he was commended by Paul in Philemon 2 as a fellow-soldier. If, however, the letter to Philemon was written first, the inference may well be that the ministry of Archippus was in danger of slipping away from him.

Whatever way the question is taken, the A.V. rendering of Colossians 4:17 is very telling, 'Archippus, take heed!' He had received a ministry from the Lord that he might fulfil it, and the Colossians were instructed to remind him of his obligation. In the Christian life, many seem to respond to the O.T. words, 'Abram, get out' or 'Joshua, go over' with much early promise, but in later life begin to sag. We may well ask, 'How much ministry world-wide lies unfulfilled?' And as we ask the question, call to mind the words, 'Archippus, take heed!'

*Walk in wisdom toward them that are without, **redeeming the time**.*
Colossians 4:5

___

The words, 'Redeeming the time' from Ephesians 5:16 and Colossians 4:5 have passed into everyday speech, with very few people being aware of their origin, and fewer still having any knowledge of the settings in which the words are found.

The reference in Ephesians 5 is linked to the Christian's walk, with the exhortation to look very carefully as to how you walk and/or to see to it that you walk carefully or accurately. The illustration of the carefulness of the cat when crossing difficult ground has a voice here; it picks its way carefully and seldom cuts its paws. The wise will walk through this world with every care and as they do, they will buy up every opportunity for spiritual profit. There is the suggestion that the spiritual eye will identify in every situation what can be turned to profit, and that profit might be a word of testimony or even a word of prayer. In addition, it must be kept in mind that every day in this world where Christ has been rejected is an evil day, and will continue to be so until He takes up the reins of government.

The reference in Colossians 4 is linked directly to an orderly walk before outsiders. The form of the words does not imply that walking in wisdom is an option, but rather emphasises an obligation. Since the word rendered 'redeeming' is a present participle, it suggests an ongoing action; every opportunity has to be identified and turned to profit. The fact too that the word is in the middle voice is a reminder that it is very much the business of everyone, with no one adopting the attitude that the exhortation is for the benefit of one's neighbour. 'Redeeming the time' is very much the business of every Christian.

What shall we then say to these things? **If God be for us,** *who* can be *against us?* Romans 8:31

With the pace of life increasing and the complexities of daily living becoming more bewildering, there is a tendency with many at times to wonder if God is really for us. There is a readiness to interpret things the wrong way and from a wrong standpoint. The oppressor seems so strong and confident, and the opposition seems to have an inexhaustible supply of power and support. The Christian, in such circumstances, can hardly be blamed for asking the question that Joshua asked at Jericho when confronted by the man with a drawn sword, 'Art thou for us, or for our adversaries?' As it happened, the answer confirmed that God was for Israel, which lifted Joshua into the good of Romans 8:31, 'If God be for us, who can be against us?'

In the present age, the absence of a direct answer to the question is, of course, a test of faith. The terror of Elisha's servant when he arose one morning and found the city encompassed by the hosts of Syria, can well be understood, 'Alas, my master, how shall we do?' 'Fear not!' Elisha replied, 'for they that be with us are more than they that be with them.' The eye of faith could see what the servant could not see until he was prayed for, that there was a mountain and chariots of fire round about Elisha.

But what does the eye of faith see today when confronted by seemingly impossible odds? It is directed to a ground which can never shift, the love of God as displayed in the gift of His Son, 'He that spared not His own Son, but delivered Him up for us all, how shall He not with Him, freely give us all things' (Rom 8:32). In the light of this, the believer can then face the problems of life with all confidence, 'If God be for us' or better, 'In view of the fact that God is for us, who can be against us?' If He spared not His Son, all else is of small moment.

14

> Brethren, if a man be overtaken in a fault, *ye which are spiritual*, restore such an one in the spirit of meekness, considering thyself, less thou also be tempted. GALATIANS 6:1

The word 'Spiritual' is a word of fairly common usage amongst Christians. It is a quality which proves to be mysterious and elusive to some, and yet to others it is a normal feature of everyday Christian life. Most believers like to consider that they are held in the esteem of others as being spiritual and would be grossly offended to be considered as carnal. How the Corinthians felt is not on record after Paul wrote to them in his first Epistle, 'I could not speak unto you as unto spiritual, but as unto carnal, even as unto babes in Christ.' They were probably cut to the heart.

While it is encouraging to be recognised by other believers as being marked by spirituality, the true test is how one is before the Lord, with thoughts and faculties harnessed to the Word and all under the control of the Spirit of God. Recognition, however, by the unsaved is another matter. The unconverted, not having the Spirit, do not have the means of reading and assessing a Christian life. Good works can be appreciated; dedication can be acknowledged, but the fruit of the Spirit, so contrary to the mind of the flesh, will always remain a mystery. Here the believer, living before the unconverted, must be content on many occasions to be justified in spirit, because the finer points of the Christian life are beyond the unsaved to understand.

The words, 'Ye which are spiritual' are from Galatians 6:1, and were written by Paul to move a certain class to answer to the address and carry out a work of restoration. How many would answer? We cannot say! Did they know the words which Paul wrote to the Corinthians, 'If any man thinketh himself to be spiritual, let him acknowledge that the things that I write unto you are the commandments of the Lord'? Possibly not the letter, but certainly the spirit of them! Which makes the Christian ponder, 'Could God count on me when the appeal goes out under the words, "Ye which are spiritual" and would I bow to His Word and move accordingly, come what may?' A very interesting thought to ponder over!

*And we know that **all things work together for good** to them that love God, to them who are the called according to His purpose.* ROMANS 8:28

his text from Romans 8:28 must rank amongst the leaders when it comes to finding comfort from the Word of God. At the same time, it has been one of the most wrongly quoted texts, being used to justify many a wrong means, albeit with a reasonably sound end in view. To follow a course of self-will and think that there will be a happy ending is stretching the meaning of the text far beyond what it was intended to bear.

Taken, however, in its setting, there are few sections of the Word of God which encompass in a few words such comfort and encouragement. Since the name of God occurs twice in some versions of the original, some translators have given the rendering, 'God works all things together for good.' This lessens the thought of the circumstances of life just clicking into position, and establishes rather the reminder that God has an interest in all those who love Him, and it is He who personally arranges life's circumstances.

Immediately preceding the text is an important revelation about prayer. Paul states that because of our weaknesses, we cannot pray aright as we do not know what the future holds and we do not know what is best for us. But the situation is not hopeless: if all we can bring to God is an inarticulate sigh, the Holy Spirit can take that up and give it meaning before God.

Immediately following the text there is a look into the past and a glimpse of the future. From the vantage point of time, those who love God can appreciate something of the eternal purposes of God in His Son for the benefit of His saints, predestinated — glorified!

So instead of being like Jacob and saying, 'All these things are against

me' (although they were not), far better to give way to the knowledge that it is in us deep down and accept that the circumstances of life are under God's control and that He works them all together in His gracious designs for the good of His saints.

*And He said unto them, **Come ye yourselves apart** into a desert place, and rest a while...* MARK 7:31

These lovely words, recorded by Mark, were spoken to the disciples by the Lord after they had completed a season of ministry; a mission not without its trials, no doubt, but not without its blessings either. Who would have thought that twelve simple men, sent forth two by two round the villages by their Lord would have accomplished so much and yet stirred up so much opposition? They might have thought as they set out, 'The task is too great and the resources are too small', but obediently they went and in a short time the word of report reached the throne of Herod. Doubt about the power given to them did not seem to enter into the situation. They simply went forth ministering according to the instructions given to them and the results were left in higher hands.

The coming back to the Lord is not without significance. The details about how much the disciples told are few, but the words, 'Told Him all things' suggest that they had great things to tell Him about their deeds and their preaching. Surely the Lord who had sent them forth would listen to every account with gladness? There are neither words of correction nor words of commendation recorded but the greatest servant of all simply said, 'Come ye yourselves apart and rest awhile.'

There is surely a principle here; a guiding example for all who would serve the Lord Christ? To tell Him all things, both said and done, suggests a condition of transparency. The Lord who knows all things anyway still wants His servants to tell Him all and so keep open the lines of trust and communion.

Only Mark records the intimacy of the invitation, 'Ye yourselves.' Not the crowds, just themselves apart with the Lord to rest. But the rest was short and the needs of the multitude disturbed it very quickly. Even now some will not take rest while there is a need and while there is strength and the will to go on; something like the great pioneer of the last century who died on duty and on his knees in prayer. It is said that when his body was finally laid to rest in Westminster Abbey, Mr Punch doffed his Jester's cap and stood in reverence to say:

> *Let marble crumble*
> *This is LIVINGstone*

The Lord Christ will not forget.

Set your affection on things above, *not on things on the earth.*
COLLOSSIANS 3:2

There is no contradiction between the exhortation of Paul to set the affections on things above and the words of the two men in white apparel recorded in Acts 1:11, 'Ye men of Galilee, why stand ye gazing up into heaven?' The setting of the affections of Colossians 3 and the earnest gaze of Acts 1 are not at odds. The challenging question in Acts 1 was for the purpose of bringing the disciples back to the reality of living, and the exhortation of Paul was for the purpose of lifting the affections above the reality of living; two quite complementary situations.

The heavenward gaze of the disciples can well be understood. After all, had the Lord not been with them at the very spot on which they stood? Had they not watched Him slowly rise from their company and ascend up on high? There must have been sorrow, indeed concern, yes, perhaps even panic, as He who had cared for them in every way ascended and left them behind on earth. Yet there seems to be something significant in the reverence to 'Ye men of Galilee.' Why that? Why Galilee? Was it not a reminder that in earlier days in Galilee they were busy men? In Galilee they were workers, and it was while they were at their work they were called to higher service with a new master. Not for them to stand on a spot for ever, however significant, or even sacred to them. There was work to be done; witnessing for the Lord in Jerusalem and district, and who better to do it than busy men who knew what work was and who had covered the territory with the Lord? It was not time for gazing up; it was time for working.

The words of exhortation to the Colossians are somewhat different. The passage could be read, 'If (as is the case) ye died with Christ, and if (as is the case), ye were raised with Christ, fix your minds on things above and not on things on the earth.' The consequence implied of having died with Christ (as all true believers have), and having been raised with Christ (as all true believers have), must be a complete break with the old habits of the past and a working out of new ones. The affections, therefore, are not to be fixed on any spot on earth; that would be a contradiction of what had taken place in a believer's life, but on Christ where He is, at the right hand of God. Died and raised must not be dismissed as positional technicalities, but challenging facts which should draw the affections away from earth so that they might be fixed on Christ. There is no profit in standing gazing up; there is work to be done. But equally important, it is vital to a believer's condition while working, to constantly be contemplating Christ where He is, at the right hand of God.

*T*his quotation from 1 Thessalonians 5:14 contains one of the great words of the New Testament, sometimes translated patience and sometimes longsuffering. From the earliest days of Christianity, commentators have waxed eloquent in dealing with this word, each striving to express a thought or definition which would bring out some new shade of meaning or some greater degree of accuracy. Such are the possibilities inherent in it, that despite all that has been written there are still great thoughts to be expressed, as much depends on the context in which it is used.

There is in English usage a word, short-tempered, and most people know what it means. Unfortunately the English language does not have a word, long-tempered, which would, to all intents and purposes, be the opposite, and which would express very well the meaning of the word rendered, patient, in 1 Thessalonians 5:14. To be short-tempered with some is understandable; to be long-tempered with some is also understandable, but to be longsuffering to all requires a grace that only comes from a Spirit-filled life.

Longsuffering (or, patience) is one of the garments with which the new man must clothe himself (Col 3:12), and it is one of the ninefold parts of the fruit of the Spirit (Gal 5). It is a basic feature of Christian love (1 Cor 13:4) and it is one of the essentials for accompanying Christian ministry (2 Tim 4:2).

In Christian service, people and events test patience. Paul asked for prayer that he might be delivered from unreasonable men; he knew very well the problems. Yet it was he more than any of the other writers who pressed the point that no matter how unreasonable men were, the believer must not lose patience, and must not lose hope for them. Longsuffering will never admit defeat, however dark and incomprehensible events and people may be.

In the wisdom of God, all the necessary graces for coping with the complexities of life were placed in the believer at conversion when the Holy Spirit entered. They are all there potentially, and given time and scope they will all come out in due measure. To know this is a great comfort; to experience the outworking of Christian graces when people or events call for anger or despair is a great encouragement. Makrothumia (as the word is) describes the character of God, 'He is longsuffering, not willing that any should perish, but that all should go on to repentance' (2 Pet 3:9). Should not the Christian display something of that grace in dealing with men and women? The Scripture says, 'Be patient toward all.'

Be careful for nothing; *but in every thing by prayer and supplication with thanksgiving let your requests be made known unto God.* PHILIPPIANS 4:6

*I*n the course of time some words change their meanings. Perhaps the words 'careful' and 'careless' come into that category. In times past one would probably be understood as being full of cares and the other as having no cares of any sort. In modern usage 'careful' in most cases would be understood as giving due consideration to people and things, whereas 'careless' would suggest a lack of consideration to the point of being heedless and unconcerned. At first sight, Paul's exhortation to the Philippians 'Be careful for nothing' would seem to give license to a life which was totally devoid of consideration, whereas what he really meant was far removed from that.

It is strange that Paul, who exhorted the Philippians not to be over-anxious about anything, used the same word to the Corinthians when he wrote of his daily anxious care for all the assemblies. Perhaps there is a concern that reflects the depths of interest that a believer should have for the things of God, whereas personal and material things ought not to have the same degree of priority of importance. In holding on to anxious care for personal reasons there is a sense of mistrusting God; of casting doubt on what He has said in His Word. Our Lord considered the matter to be of such importance that He dealt with it in His sermon on the mount (Mt 6). When He said, 'Take no thought' He used the same word that Paul used to the Philippians (Be not over-anxious). He did not mean a complete indifference to everything but rather a peaceful trust; a confidence in His Father's care for the individual. The Saviour also used the same word when He counselled Martha for being careful and troubled about many things; the things about the house which could very well wait for another time, but the 'good part' of Mary's choice could not.

Although Philippians 4:6 discourages over-anxiety it encourages prayer and therefore a seeking of the presence of God. To bring repeatedly a foreboding anxiety into the presence of God would certainly be out of place, indeed Peter put the matter into perspective in his words, 'Having cast all your care (same word) upon Him' — a once-for-all transaction. There is something, however, that can be brought into the presence of God with prayer, and that is thanksgiving. One excellent commentator has said, 'To pray in any other spirit is to clip the wings of prayer.'

*Put on therefore, as **the elect of God,** holy and beloved, bowels of mercies, kindness, humbleness of mind, meekness, longsuffering...* COLOSSIANS 3:12

*A*mongst the many names by which Christians are known, 'Elect of God' must be about the most wonderful. To consider the past, 'chosen in Him before the foundation of the world'; to think of the future, 'what manner of people ought ye to be...looking for and hastening the coming of the day of God'; it is hardly a matter of surprise that for the present there should be a most practical application, 'Put on therefore as the elect of God, holy and beloved, bowels of mercies, kindness, humbleness of mind, meekness, longsuffering' (Col 3:12).

'Elect' is not a New Testament word exclusively. In Isaiah 42:1, 'Behold My Servant, whom I uphold; mine elect, in whom my soul delighteth,' the title is applied to the Lord in the section of the book which deals with prophecies of peace. Although the context of Isaiah 42 was obviously lost on the Jews, the title was not, as before the cross they cried, 'He saved others, let him save himself if he be the Christ, the elect of God.' The action of the mob, however, was not ignored by heaven, as Peter makes known in majestic words, 'I lay in Zion a chief corner stone, elect, precious, and he that believeth on Him shall not be confounded.' He was, 'disallowed indeed of men, but chosen (elect) of God, and precious.'

But where is the lesson today? Apart from the graces the believer is exhorted to put on, there is the wonderful thought of being involved in the eternal plans of God. The God of heaven has taken up men and women to make known His mind to the world, truly indeed, 'living epistles.' One would hardly have thought that in being associated with the eternal plans of God, the graces listed in Colossians 3:12 would have told out much of the character of the God of eternity, but they do, and that is a source of wonder in itself.

Notice the verse does not say, 'put on holiness'. That condition is a fact from God's side, 'holy and beloved'! What grace, unearned and undeserved, that

men and women should be so described, who were alienated from God by wicked works! Who would not wish to tell out something of the character of such a God, by putting on as His elect, bowels of mercies, kindness, humbleness of mind, meekness, longsuffering? Who knows, perhaps then, at least in measure, will come to pass what Isaiah said in his manifesto those many years ago, 'And in His Name shall the Gentiles trust.'

'I will have mercy on whom I will have mercy,

and I will have compassion

on whom I will have compassion.'

What shall we say then? *Shall we continue in sin, that grace may abound?* ROMANS 6:1

There is a very interesting question in the Epistle to the Romans which keeps cropping up. The question is, 'What shall we say then?' or, on some occasions in an expanded form, 'What shall we say then to these things?' The writer, in the unfolding of his arguments, seems to feel the need of asking at certain points, 'What can we deduce from the things I have set out?', and then he proceeds to answer the question he has raised. A classical example is found at Romans 6:1, where the question is posed, 'What shall we say then? Shall we continue in sin that grace may abound?' The answer is quickly given, 'God forbid (by no means), how shall we that died to sin live any longer therein?' The incompatibility of death and life together demands the conclusion that continuing in sin is an impossibility.

Another classical example is found at chapter 8:31, following an unfolding of God's dealings with His saints from predestination through to the ultimate of glorification. The question is asked, 'What shall we say then to these things?' This is followed by another question; a question which has brought strength and courage to millions since Paul posed it. 'If God be for us, who can be against us?' Even if the answer were not given (and it is, thankfully), the very form of the words in the question should remove all doubts and give assurance to all who believe in God, that the adversary has no power when God takes up His people's cause. But if any created intelligence should have the temerity to challenge the givingness or righteousness of God, all He requires to do is to point to Calvary, 'He that spared not His own Son, but delivered Him up for us all, how shall He not with Him freely give us all things?' There is the proof, if proof is needed, of the limitless interest of God in all His saints.

But God's servants do not challenge the character of God. They are happy with the answer to the question raised at chapter 9:14, 'What shall we say then? Is there unrighteousness with God?' God forbid (by no means). For He said to Moses, 'I will have mercy on whom I will have mercy, and I will have compassion on whom I will have compassion.' The most insignificant of His saints (and who would claim to be more?) is not beyond support. What shall we say then to these things?

In every thing give thanks: *for this is the will of God in Christ Jesus* *concerning you.* 1 Thessalonians 5:18

This little exhortation from 1 Thessalonians 5:18 is about the most difficult one in the Scriptures to put into practice. To be able to identify a cause for thanksgiving in every event of life, especially the adverse ones, calls for an exceptional standard of spirituality. Many believers would recognise in adversity a cause for giving up, rather than one for thanksgiving. Perhaps that is why there is so much sympathy for Elijah when he sat down under the juniper tree and requested for himself that he might die. Life had become such a disappointment to him; things had gone so wrong that death seemed the only way out. How gracious of his God that He did not take Elijah at his word; and anyway He had more for His servant to do. The fact that Elijah was a man subject to like passions as we are, seems to make us all want to identify with him when the pressure of living for God in a godless world comes upon us.

But Paul's exhortation in 1 Thessalonians 5:18 was not a pious hope; he added very telling words, 'for this is the will of God concerning you.' This is God's gracious design in Christ for His people. The fact that our Lord gave thanks when faced with rejection, 'I thank Thee O Father ... for so it was well-pleasing in Thy sight' must surely be an encouragement to His followers. The adversity was not pleasant but He gave thanks because He knew that in His acceptance of the situation the Father's will was being accomplished.

Perhaps the secret of the exhortation is to be found in the knowledge of doing the Father's will when giving thanks in everything. This is what He wants; it brings so much pleasure to Him. Paul moved in the good of that. More than once he wrote, 'I am bound to give thanks' or more accurately, 'I am a debtor to give

thanks.' The good hand of God in evidence all around him constituted him a debtor, and the only way he could discharge the debt was to give thanks to God.

Thanksgiving, when regarded as one aspect of prayer should never be absent from any of our devotions. It will subsist in heaven, according to R. C. Trench, but fuller and richer there because only then will it be known how much is owed to the Lord.

Charity suffereth long, and is kind; charity envieth not; charity vaunteth not itself, is not puffed up, Doth not behave itself unseemly, seeketh not her own, is not easily provoked, thinketh no evil; Rejoiceth not in iniquity, but rejoiceth in the truth; Beareth all things, believeth all things, hopeth all things, endureth all things. **Charity never faileth** ... 1 Corinthians 13:4–8

For many, 1 Corinthians 13 is the most beautiful chapter in the New Testament. Believing it to be so, it also has to be remembered that it is one of the most demanding chapters; it is a test of faith and it demands self-examination. The short section from verse 4 to verse 7 is not just fourteen ideas strung together; it is a very carefully set-out rhythm of seven couplets, setting out some of the characteristics of love from God's side, and culminating in the categorical statement of verse 8, 'Love never faileth.'

An examination of the couplets, so beautifully balanced in themselves, must, for space reasons, be outside the scope of this short meditation. The conclusion, however, has within its three words the capability of imprinting the message of the couplets firmly in the mind. No allowance is made for doubts; no condition in life can possibly affect the conclusion, 'Love never faileth.'

If the word 'love' were used in the frame of its ordinary English usage, the statement, 'Love never faileth' would not be true; indeed it would hardly make sense. For the Christian, happily, there is a word reserved by the Holy Spirit, which speaks of an energy which has its roots in God. Although the word for love was discarded by the world of Paul's day, God took it up and gave it a meaning quite outside the understanding of man, and so we read something of its depth in those majestic yet mysterious words, 'For God so loved the world.' It was a world of unlovable men and women, but God chose to set His love upon it nevertheless. That love faileth **never** – a little adverb of negation, saying, 'Not at any time, not once or ever,' 'Love never **faileth**.' Peter uses the third word in his first Epistle when he states, 'The grass withereth and the flower thereof falleth away.' When the green of summer turns to autumn gold the flower falls. When the leaf of the tree drops, as far as the tree is concerned the leaf has fallen out of existence. But love is not like that, it never falls away, it never fails, it will outwear everything, it will never cease to exist. For the Christian there must never be a doubt about the love of God; it has its roots in Him; it is just as eternal as He is, and the Scripture is true, 'Love never faileth.'

*Finally, brethren, whatsoever things are true, whatsoever things are honest, whatsoever things are just, whatsoever things are pure, whatsoever things are lovely, whatsoever things are of good report; if there be any virtue, and if there be any praise, **think on these things**.* PHILIPPIANS 4:8

*N*ever at any time in human history has the mind been subjected to such a barrage of damaging material as in the present day, and it is therefore most pertinent to lay hold of an exhortation of the past; one which is never out of date, 'think on these things.'

This very challenging call comes at the end of a short list of virtues. It must not be construed as a call for mere mental reflection; good as that may be on occasions. What Paul is obviously meaning is the calculated thought which will produce an altered conduct of life. This is clearly borne out in the exhortation of the next verse, 'these things do.' Such is christian living and that is what the Epistle to the Philippians is all about.

Here then in Philippians 4:8 are six adjectives describing christian ideals. From an examination of other lists of virtues and graces in the New Testament, it is clear that this one is different. The six words form parameters, within which the believer can find refuge. As the virtues are adopted in daily living there is manifested a dignity, the prestige of which is much sought after by many, but which is so elusive. The secret lies of course in the Christian's ability to give the virtues their proper expression. Without Christ and the power of the indwelling Spirit it is impossible to gain the benefit of the preservation, and equally impossible to project the high standards of the christian life.

So Paul sums up by using a word he does not use elsewhere. 'If there be any virtue (whatever excellence there is), and if there be any praise (whatever might call down the approval of God), think on these things.'

God has done His part. In Philippians 4:7 there is the declaration, as a free translation has it, 'And the peace of God, which is beyond our wildest dreams, shall garrison your hearts and minds through Christ Jesus.' It is all very well to exult over what God has done, is doing, and will yet do, but bending the mind to consider what is of moral excellence is quite another matter. What shall we do then? Let us take Paul's exhortation in Philippians 4:8, 'Think on these things.'

> *And Abner had communication with the elders of Israel, saying, Ye sought for David in times past to be king over you:* **Now then do it**: *for the* LORD *hath spoken of David, saying, By the hand of my servant David I will save my people Israel…* 2 SAMUEL 3:17–18

*T*his very striking piece of advice is taken from the words of Abner to the Elders of Israel, as recorded in 2 Samuel 3:17–18, 'Ye sought for David in times past to be king over you; NOW THEN, DO IT: for the Lord hath spoken of David saying, "By the hand of my servant David I will save my people Israel…"'

Abner is not generally remembered for his wise counsel; he is remembered more for his political intrigue and for the way he died, summed up in the well-known words of David, 'Died Abner as a fool dieth?' With all his faults, he nevertheless recognised that David's star was on the ascendancy and his counsel to the elders was first-rate. The time for hesitating was past. The way forward was clear. David must be crowned king. NOW THEN, DO IT!

Sometimes caution, mixed with a lack of faith, causes believers to hesitate when the pathway is clearly marked. On occasions the cost of a decision to move is considered to be too great; or the resources are thought to be too small, or the problem seems to be too big, and so many a work for the Lord is not done. Perhaps Abner's words, 'now then, do it,' have a voice for all who know there is a work to be undertaken for the Lord, but for whatever reason, they have not carried it out.

By nature, many of God's people are pessimists. That leap into the dark, as it were, is too much to take; things might go wrong. In matters which are spiritual, there may be perhaps a lack of vision, or even a lack of trust. Of course, if the way forward is not clear then obviously Abner's words do not apply. If however, there are no obvious reasons for reluctance, loss may result in holding back.

David's Lord and greater Son is very often the subject of similar circumstances. The gospel preacher will readily find a parallel in the thought of making haste to crown the Saviour King of kings. But to some believers, the initial transaction in salvation is made to suffice for life and the constant exalting of the Saviour and the desire to do His work daily, loses all sense of urgency. Is there a work for our hands to do? Is there an open door to go through? If so, surely the words of Abner are most applicable, NOW THEN, DO IT!

*And the apostles said unto the Lord, **increase our faith**.* Luke 17:15

 n the opening words of Luke 17, dealing with forgiveness for those who constantly err, the disciples interpreted the situation as one which required an increase of faith to deal with it. It might have been better if they had asked for an increase of forbearance or something of that nature; but no, they asked for an increase of faith. At first sight, this request of the apostles seems to be most commendable. 'Add to our faith' must surely be the language of those intent on deepening their appreciation of spiritual things.

What follows in the context of Luke 17 does not seem to support the disciples; in fact, the Saviour seems to say to them, 'You are on the wrong track. If you have faith, even though it is as small as a grain of mustard seed and you act in the good of it you could do what is naturally impossible; you could uproot a tree and replant it in the sea.'

What follows from the Lord seems to be a kind of safeguard, lest by exercising faith the servant is lifted up in pride by the results. In the strange little parable, if such it is, the disciples are reminded that they are in the service of God. In the ordinary affairs of life, a master would not say to his slave, 'Have your own meal first and then serve me.' Rather he would say, 'Serve me first and then attend to yourself.' The master is not placed under a debt to his servant, it is all in a day's work; the service is rendered by the slave as a matter of course.

In the service of God there must never be the attitude by what has been done, God has been placed under a servant's debt. There must never be the attitude that the past has been so splendidly performed that the servant has a right to put his own needs first. In other words, in the setting of the parable, the servant cannot say to his master, 'I served you well yesterday, now you can wait until I have eaten and then I shall attend to you.'

Service for God, in whatever sphere, is not improved by asking God to make up for a deficiency of faith. That would be tantamount to putting the blame on God for the shortfall, if such it was thought to be. It is not a question of probing into what motivates God in relation to His servants, but rather, a recognition of what spirit should motivate the servant as the heavy demands of God's service are identified. God will support His servants' faith, though it be as small as a grain of mustard seed. Perhaps if God's servants were to walk more in the light of that, they would be able to take up old Caleb's words, 'Now therefore, give me this mountain.'

'Serve me first and then attend to yourself.'

his exhortation from the pen of Paul would seem to place an intolerable burden upon believers. Even in the less complex days of the first century, the Thessalonians must have baulked at it at first reading. At face value the exhortation would seem to suggest an ongoing enquiry into every facet of daily life, and in the 20th century, with all its complexities, that would seem to be an unacceptably heavy demand. Of course, Paul was quite aware of the pressures of the world system all around him and his fellow-saints. Indeed to one assembly he wrote that there were many voices clamouring to be heard and none of them was without signification. And no doubt, as the centuries have rolled on, the voices have not grown less in number, indeed there is every possibility that they are more diverse; certainly more intensified.

How then, in a world such as it is, will the Christian prove all things? Well, firstly, it may be that the exhortation is connected with the one which goes before it, and if so, it would then read, 'Despise not prophesyings but prove all things.' Now that would narrow the field somewhat and would mean that there should be an examination, a proving, a testing of every communication put before the people. But supposing the connection is not there, what then? Either way the Christian must realise that there really is a need to apply spiritual discernment to each unfolding circumstances of life. To enable the believer to do this the necessary wherewithal has been imparted. Every child of God was given the ability when the Spirit of God entered and potentially all that is required is there if He is in residence. It is simply then a matter of spiritual growth as each succeeding day comes with its challenges and spiritual discernment is applied. Some circumstances are identified for prayer, some for praise, some for action of one kind or another, and of course, some to be shunned.

In mentioning the wherewithal given to Christians to prove all things in the journey through life, the value of the Holy Scriptures must not be under-rated. Without a knowledge of the Word and recourse to it in certain circumstances, spiritual discernment would be a very difficult exercise. The ability therefore to identify what is good and what is bad, what is right and what is wrong has been taken care of by God. The Holy Spirit and the Word of God are there to serve and to help every child of God to prove all things and therefore to hold fast to that which is good.

*And we desire that every one of you do shew the same diligence to the **full assurance of hope** unto the end.* HEBREWS 6:11

*T*he expression 'the full assurance of hope' is found in Hebrews 6:11. The word behind 'full assurance' only occurs four times in the New Testament, but each occurrence carries a considerable weight of meaning, as in Colossians 2:2, 1 Thessalonians 1:5 and Hebrews 10:22. To the Hebrew who had embraced Christianity but was having second thoughts, even doubts, the encouragement to have full assurance of hope in the soul needed something solid to pin that hope upon. The hymn-writer's words, 'some build their hopes on the ever-drifting sands' would sum up the attitude of the godless, but that is not what marks out the believer. The soul is like a ship, being tossed to and fro on the sea of life, and it needs an anchor that will not drag, and a foundation that is firm and true. Happily the anchor for the soul is not fixed to the ocean bed, but in the heights above, within the veil in the heavenly sanctuary, even on God Himself.

The word for anchor occurs four times in the New Testament. Three of the four occurrences refer to Paul's voyage which ended in shipwreck, but the sole remaining mention of the word, used figuratively, carries with it the assurance that there is no possibility of movement. The hope held out to the Hebrews is an anchor that is fixed within the veil.

In Hebrews 6, God is seen to have established two great facts, firstly with Abraham and then with believers in this age. These two facts, His word and His oath are given as evidences that God cannot lie. There is no movement there, no vacillating, no turning back, no retraction. These are, in the words of Scripture, two immutable things and are given that believers might have strong consolation. That strong consolation is the cable which connects the soul to the anchor and that anchor is fastened within the veil. Nothing could be more sure and steadfast, and let us not forget, the forerunner has entered in already. It is not surprising, therefore, that with all the evidence given to remove all doubts, that the writer to the Hebrews should pull out a special word and call for 'full assurance of hope.'

But *my God* shall supply all *your need* according to His riches in glory by Christ Jesus. PHILIPPIANS 4:19

---

*T*he phrase 'Your need — my God' is a reversal of the order given in Philippians 4:19, but since most people see their need before they acknowledge God, perhaps the order given, 'Your need — my God' is nearer the truth in the experience of the majority of believers. The order of the words in the original reads, 'And the God of me, will fill every need of you', and although it is not good English as rendered, it certainly makes good sense.

One wonders why Paul chose to be so possessive in saying, 'My God.' Would he not have been more charitable in saying, 'Our God' or 'Your God'? On reflection, there is a sense in which personal possessiveness of this nature takes precedence over other considerations, such as seen in the language of Thomas, 'My Lord and my God', or the words of Mary in the garden. 'They have taken away my Lord.' The fact that others had the same claim did not seem to matter, eyes and heart were fixed on Him. The answer to Paul's possessiveness is of course in the context. He spoke from his experiences of the faithfulness of God; he was never let down, never empty, always content, and now he records, 'I have all things, I am full.'

There is a word in the New Testament for, 'supply' which carries with it the idea of lavish abundance. Peter uses it, for example in his first Epistle, chapter 4, 'Of the ability which God supplieth.' But Paul does not use that word in Philippians 4:19, although one would have expected it. He uses a word which means, 'to fill up.' The sense of it is caught so tellingly in Moule's paraphrase, 'I cannot requite you, but my God shall fill up every need of yours, making up to you in His own loving providence the gap in your means left by this your bounty.' Yes, He will draw on no less a treasury than that of 'His Glory' … in Christ Jesus, in whom all fulness dwells!

It is good to be reminded that the gap left by giving to God, becomes His responsibility to replace, and He will do it now from His abundant resources in Heaven, and He will not forget to add to that in the coming glory.

Paul, of course, is absolutely correct, the order should not be, 'Your need, my God' but 'My God, your need.' God is never behind in matters which affect His saints.

. . . . he was never let down, never empty, always
content, and now he records, 'I have all things,
I am full.'

It has often been remarked that the home at Bethany was a very special and hallowed spot to the Lord. There was warmth, sincerity and reality there; conditions which the Saviour appreciated, and indeed needed in His short earthly sojourn. The crowds with whom He had to mix were so fickle; one day desirous of making Him a king and the next demanding from Him a sign to prove He had really come from God. But Bethany was different, no signs were needed there. The words, 'Lord if thou hadst been here my brother had not died', tell it all.

Yet in that special home, Martha in a remonstrating sort of way, asks, 'Dost Thou not care?' It was the same form of words as used by the disciples in the storm, 'Carest Thou not that we perish?' In both cases the question can read, 'Does it not matter to you?' They seem to say, 'You can see our plight, and you have the answer, but does it not matter to you?' How many times in one's short life has such a cry been made? Christians forget the words of Peter, or worse, they may choose to forget them when life's problems assume proportions that are larger than the faith of the moment. Peter's words are true words, 'He careth for you.'

From another point of view, how many have any feeling for the Lord when His loving care is challenged? On the human plane when one who loves has that love questioned there is hurt and disappointment. In such circumstances it would seem that one's problems have found a gap in another's care and that provides the entitlement to ask, 'Does it not matter to you?' How must the Lord feel when His saints take up this stance, 'Dost Thou not care?'

Of course the Saviour cares. What must be learned in life, albeit so difficult at times to accept, is how and when the Lord will intervene. He had a better portion for Martha if only she would take it, and He was, after all, in the same boat as the disciples; their problem was His problem. Referring again to Peter's words about casting all our cares (anxieties) on Him, it is not generally appreciated that the literal rendering from the original of the latter half of 1 Peter 5:7, reads, 'Because to Him it matters concerning you.' Does that not answer the question, 'Dost Thou not care, does it not matter to you?'

*W*hen the Lord rose from supper and girded Himself with a towel to carry out His last act of service to His disciples, the scripture says, 'then cometh He to Simon Peter.' The disciples who had received His gracious ministry of feet-washing accepted it in silent wonder, but Peter, impetuous as ever, had three comments to make.

    1)   'Lord, dost thou wash my feet?'
    2)   'Thou shalt never wash my feet.'
    3)   'Lord, not my feet only.'

To the first question, the Lord answers, 'What I do thou knowest not now; but thou shalt know hereafter.' In other words, the full significance of the feet-washing was reserved for a future day, it was not simply an act of humility.

To the next statement, 'Thou shalt never wash my feet,' the Lord replied, 'If I wash thee not, thou hast no part with me.' He did not say, 'no part in me,' that would refer to the great work of the cross, which, once accomplished, would never need to be repeated. 'Part with me' in feet-washing signifies the removal by the Lord of everything that dulls our spirits, that chills our souls, that hinders communion; in fact everything that hinders part with Christ. It is not strictly His work as Advocate, as that deals with sins, or His ministry as High Priest, as that deals principally with our infirmities, although there may be a bit of both involved, but it symbolises His present ministry of removing from the spirits of His saints, everything that would hinder part with Him.

As the pendulum swings to the other extreme, Peter's third remark, 'Lord, not my feet only, but also my hands and my head' draws from the Lord the wondrous truth, 'He that is bathed (washed all over), needeth not save to wash his feet, but is clean every whit.' Only once is a person 'washed all over,' and that is at conversion; it never requires to be repeated, but in the believer's journey through this world, contamination of some kind or another is unavoidable. For this, the great work of the Saviour is on-going all the time. To refuse to submit to His gracious ministry must draw the same words as were addressed to Peter, 'Thou hast no part with me.' To carry on in service with broken communion with the Lord, and a chilled soul as a result, is a great grief to the One who in the past took the towel, and who carries on the same ministry today for all His saints.

And in that day ye shall ask Me nothing. Verily, verily, I say unto you, Whatsoever ye shall ask the Father in My name, He will give it you.
JOHN 16:23

*I*n the Gospel by John there are eight discourses or sermons of the Lord; four of them delivered in the presence of men and women generally and four of them to the disciples only. In the eighth and final sermon recorded in John 16, which could be entitled 'world witnessing' there is a very telling little section. It is found in verses 23 and 24 of John 16, and it speaks of a new day about to dawn. It is from this section of the Word that the title of this short meditation is drawn, a reference to the future, 'In that day.'

The new day of which the Saviour spoke to His disciples concerned communication. Up to this point the disciples could address their enquiries to Him, but now He said, 'In that day, ye shall ask me nothing.' This is not to be interpreted as meaning that they were never again to address the Lord but rather that new lines of communication would be opened up with direct access to the Father. They had known this before. It was as Martha stated, 'I know that…whatsoever thou wilt ask of God, God will give it thee.' But in the new day things would be different. There would be no need to appeal to the Lord to go to the Father on their behalf; it was open to them to ask the Father direct and do it in the Name of Christ.

The new day has dawned. To the disciples it was introduced as being in the future, although not very far into the future. 'In that day' they could request in His Name and it would be granted and they would have fulness of joy. The great pity is that in this present day the privileges of the new day intimated by the Lord are lightly esteemed; access to the Father carries little feeling of awe and wonder; requesting in His Name is not a priority, and so, fulness of joy is lost. The importance of the new day with its privileges has been lost to most. Although the news of it was introduced by the words, 'Verily, verily' to intimate that they were words of Deity; words which had never before fallen on mortal ear; words which once given would never be withdrawn, they have not been taken to heart. Therein lies our misfortune. The resources of heaven are largely untapped because the privileges of 'that day' which is now 'this day' have not been appreciated. But perhaps there is still time to take them up.

Walk in wisdom *toward them that are without, redeeming the time.*
COLOSSIANS 4:5

The little exhortation 'walk in wisdom' from Colossians 4:5 reads in the original, 'In wisdom walk ye', putting wisdom in the place of prominence.

There is little doubt that most Christians would readily agree with Paul that wisdom is an essential quality for a proper walk before the unsaved, and having agreed, would pass on to read the rest of the verse and perhaps the rest of the chapter. But what is wisdom in the biblical sense? Does it deserve closer examination? After all, James teaches that there is a wisdom which does not come from above, which is earthly, soulish and devilish. It has no other horizon but earth, it is marked by animal cunning and it produces the kind of situation the devil delights in. Now, obviously Paul did not call for that; to be motivated by that kind of wisdom before the unsaved would be courting disaster.

What then is wisdom? Someone has described it as the power to discern between good and evil, the ability to give advice on the practical issues of life and conduct. But then, when Paul said 'In wisdom walk ye' he surely did not imply that a man or a woman had this wisdom intuitively? No, he knew it came from above and he assumed it would be shaped by the scriptures, since the wherewithal is woven into the very fabric of the Word. Happily James has condensed that and in his Epistle gives eight or nine marks of the wisdom which comes from above. Motivated by these qualities or virtues, the Christian's walk before the unsaved will have a very telling impact.

There is, however, a very searching tailpiece to Paul's exhortation. The brevity of time forces him to add the words, 'redeeming the time.' Now, what is he saying? Is it not the need to identify every circumstance of life as an opportunity to serve the Lord? Is it not an encouragement to buy out of the market of life what can be purchased or salvaged for God? Here is an encouragement to see men and women in the face of every clock, on the page of every calendar, since time is swiftly passing by. Every hour of every day is a reminder that opportunities are slipping past unless they are bought up for God. Let then the unsaved see in christian living the marks of the wisdom that is from above. It is beyond their powers to understand, but in the power of the Spirit it will have a telling effect.

For consider Him that endured such contradiction of sinners against himself,
lest ye be wearied *and faint in your minds.* Hebrews 12:3

The force of the expression 'lest ye be wearied' can well be understood in respect to Hebrews who were finding the going hard. Standing firm when pressures on every side were being applied to force a return to the old way of life, was a very wearing experience. It could very well lead to a fainting of the soul, as Hebrews 12:3 makes plain. On a wider application, bearing testimony for the Lord; just being faithful to Him in a hostile world has the same effect at times. Weariness creeps in. Losing heart is a common outcome.

It would seem that the writer to the Hebrews was suggesting that he knew of the pressures, but before weariness set in, and in consequence, a serious spiritual enfeeblement, it would be to their salvation to compare their problems with what the Saviour experienced. Here is the answer, the secret, the key to the whole matter, 'Consider Him!' There was something in the Saviour's experience which nerved Him for the conflict. What was that? 'The joy that was set before Him.' And what was the outcome? 'He endured the contradiction of sinners against Himself.'

Harassment is not a pleasant experience. Favour with the people is far more congenial but in the end may be less productive if it is a symptom of apathy concerning spiritual matters. The waxing weary of Hebrews 12:3 is the result of pressures which take their toll and cause doubts to arise about the ability to cope. If it is of any comfort, the problem is not a new one, the Saviour passed that way Himself and it may not do too much despite to the text to suggest that He would say to any so affected, 'Consider me, lest ye be wearied, ye have not yet resisted unto blood, striving against sin.'

Think on this. The Saviour in His life exercised power over demons, disease and death. He had power to control the elements and much more besides. When it came to the contradiction of sinners against Himself, the power He exercised was that of endurance, something within the scope of His saints to show when under similar pressure. Let us therefore consider Him and endure to the end.

'If it is of any comfort, the problem is not a new one,

the Saviour passed that way Himself.'

*And Peter called to mind the word that Jesus said unto him, **Before the cock crow** twice, thou shalt deny Me thrice. And when he thought thereon, he wept.* MARK 14:72

*P*eter's denial is recorded by all four Evangelists. Their accounts differ in detail, even to the point of giving material to the sceptics to claim that the differences amount to contradictions. Such is not the case; the harmony of the four accounts can be traced throughout. Much is said about Peter's boasts, 'I am ready to go with thee, both to prison and to death', 'I will lay down my life for thy sake' ('likewise said they all'), but seldom is the significance of what the Lord said to Peter considered. What did the Lord say? He said three things:

This night
Before the cock crow (Mark adds, 'twice')
Thou shalt deny me thrice

The high priest's house, the fire, the damsel, the bystanders, the oaths;

all these were incidental. What came home to Peter that night, and it had to be that night, was what is so graphically recorded by Mark, 'and the cock crew.' Then the words of the Lord came to him, but too late, he had denied the Master three times.

From that house Peter fled into the darkness, but the darkness was not an escape from himself. What he thought as he ran is not recorded. Perhaps it was the denial, perhaps total amazement at the accuracy of the Lord's words. Speculation is dangerous, but what is certain is that if the Lord could be right even to the call of a cockerel, He must be right in everything else.

How often in life, in the midst of complex circumstances, a simple occurrence like the one recorded by Mark, 'and the cock crew' brings home the challenge of whether we are standing for the truth or supporting the lie. In the challenge to Peter, 'Art thou not one of the man's disciples?', the truth is personified. By denying any knowledge of Christ, he denied the truth associated with His person. The lie was clearly conveyed to his accusers, 'I know not the man.'

Are there lessons here for Christians? One obvious one is that God does not need to write His message in the sky when a cockerel can accomplish the same purpose. Another one must surely be that if the word of Christ dwells within, His voice will be heard in the simple circumstances of life. And a third one must be that despite boasting and failure, the truth can register. The One who said, 'before the cock crow' also said, 'when thou art converted strengthen thy brethren.'

'I will lay down my life

for thy sake'

'He that spared not His own Son,

but delivered him up for us all,

how shall he not with him also

freely give us all things?'

And Jacob their father said unto them, Me have ye bereaved of my children: Joseph is not, and Simeon is not, and ye will take Benjamin away: **all these things are against me.** GENESIS 42:36

*T*he well-known words of Jacob in Genesis 42, 'Joseph is not, and Simeon is not, and ye will take Benjamin away; all these things are against me' were wrung from his heart in his anguish when his sons told him that Benjamin was to return with them to Egypt. His turmoil of soul can be well understood. Already he had lost Joseph (as he thought), the son of Rachel, and now he was faced with a demand for Rachel's other son, Benjamin. Simeon was a hostage and he had only the word of a man in Egypt that he would be released; the terms of which were more than he could face.

As all the facts are on the page of Scripture, Jacob frequently comes under heavy criticism for his lack of faith in God. His sons were alive and in good health; his fears were therefore unfounded. After all, was there not a time when he had carefully considered Joseph's dreams? Had he forgotten? Why had he let the cares of this life swamp him? When in possession of all the facts, it is comparatively easy to condemn, but take away the knowledge and it becomes a very different story.

In certain circumstances in life, men and women are prepared to believe the worst. The disciples in the boat in the storm thought they saw a phantom approach over the waters; but it was the Lord. The two on the road to Emmaus had heavy hearts as they turned away from Jerusalem; the One in whom they had pinned their hopes had gone and so all was lost. But it was not so, the stranger who joined them caused their hearts to burn within them when He took away their fears.

God's saints are not immune from thinking, 'all these things are against me.' They may not falter as much or as often as those who have no hope, but they stumble nevertheless, some to a greater degree than others. Quiet confidence in God may dwell in Job and in Mary of Bethany and in many more like them, but all too many are conscious of their doubts; fearing the worst comes too readily to the fore.

What is the answer? How can 'all these things are against me' be changed to 'all these things are for me'? The answer may be in the words of Romans 8:32, 'He that spared not His own Son, but delivered him up for us all, how shall he not with him also freely give us all things?' And if this is the case, is it a correct attitude to consider giving up in despair?

*He shall cover thee with His feathers, and **under His wings** shalt thou trust: His truth shall be thy shield and buckler.* PSALM 91:4

The author of Psalm 91 is unknown, but Satan knew its teaching and quoted from it in what is known as the temptation in the wilderness. He used it in an endeavour to tempt the Lord to stray from the path of dependence on God.

Although the background of this beautiful Psalm is not clear, its message is full of encouragement, especially verses 4 – 6 in which we find the comforting words 'under his wings'.

On the dark side there are four terrors mentioned in the three verses:

1)   The terror by night
2)   The arrow that flieth by day
3)   The pestilence that walketh in darkness
4)   The destruction that wasteth at noonday

On the bright side, before the four terrors are detailed, there are four points that have to be taken into account:

1)   He shall cover thee with his feathers
2)   Under his wings shalt thou trust
3)   His truth shall be thy shield and buckler
4)   Thou shalt not be afraid

Each day of pilgrimage contains a variety of trials and tribulations. The Psalmist lists them in a fashion which suggests that there is no time of the day when one can say that this is the hour when a believer is immune. By night there is terror and pestilence; by day there is the flying arrow or the destruction that wasteth. To the Psalmist, all these were real; they were meaningful and fraught with danger. In the language of his day he described them, and although in a different age the terrors seem different in form, they are, nevertheless, just as menacing.

What can be said? Does God provide a refuge? The Psalmist was convinced that He did and he employed a variety of figures to make clear that the everlasting God was a very present help in times of trouble.

Having to contend with all that life brings upon the Christian, there is need for a refuge, a retreat that is available day and night, a place to which the oppressed can flee. Where is that to be found? Perhaps the title of this short meditation from Psalm 91 will point in the right direction; it is 'Under His wings.'

Under His wings, what a refuge in sorrow

How the heart yearningly turns to its rest

Often when earth has no balm for my healing

There I find comfort and there I find rest.

'The darkness recedes
as the thought of His glory
grips the Psalmist's soul.'

But Thou art the same, *and Thy years shall have no end.* PSALM 102:27

*I*n Hebrews 1 there is a lengthy quotation from Psalm 102, a small part of which are the words 'Thou art the same'. The force of the quote in the Hebrew Epistle is to establish the superiority of Christ over angels. All things may change, including angels, since they too are the works of His hands, but there is no change with Christ. In the Hebrews He is addressed, 'But Thou art the same, and Thy years shall not fail.' Apart from the argument in the context of the Epistle to the Hebrews, it should certainly be a comfort to all believers who read it, that they have an unchanging God.

Psalm 102, however, is a very different setting. It has the title, 'A prayer of the afflicted when he is overwhelmed and poureth out his complaint before the Lord.' This makes the Psalm most suitable as a meditation for those who are suffering affliction and who need to be encouraged. It is one of seven penitential Psalms. Not so much a lamenting over personal guilt, but a mourning over the shortcomings of others. It divides itself into two parts; the first eleven verses dealing with the Psalmist's laments and the sorrow which weighs so heavily upon him. Indeed, so dark is the picture, that one has entitled it, 'Amidst the encircling gloom.' It is from this Psalm that the well-known words are taken, 'I am like a pelican in the wilderness, an owl in the desert, and a sparrow in the housetop.' All of these selected by the Psalmist to stress his loneliness in trial and sorrow.

The second half of the Psalm is entirely different. There is a vision of the Lord and His eternal existence. The darkness recedes as the thought of His glory grips the Psalmist's soul, 'For He hath looked down from the height of His sanctuary.' The whole Psalm has been compared to a day, which, opening with wind and rain, clears up at noon and is warm with the sun, continues fine, with intervening showers, and finally closes with a brilliant sunset.

It is from the brilliant sunset that the words are taken, 'Thou art the same.' With God's creatures, they live in constantly changing circumstances, not all of which may be convenial. But with God it is not so. He remains the same from eternity to eternity and it is with the unchanging God that His people have to do. It is therefore right to have confidence in Him. He is the same, and His years cannot fail.

And when they had brought their ships to land, they forsook all, and followed Him. LUKE 5:11 **I go a fishing.** JOHN 21:2

The words of Peter when he said 'I go a-fishing' should be considered with Luke 5:11, 'they forsook all and followed Him.' On that occasion, when they cast the nets for the last time before setting out to be fishers of men, the haul was so great that the nets broke. Such was the background of what Peter left; in its day, a most flourishing and lucrative business. But Christ eclipsed everything in him and around him and when He said, 'follow me' there was not a moment's hesitation, Peter forsook all and followed Him.

There came another day in Peter's life. A day which followed his collapse, his contrition, his confession, and happily his restoration. This was a different background to the one when he heard the call to follow. This time he was to go into Galilee and wait, and there, he and the others would see the Lord. But the Lord kept them waiting. Could they wait and watch, or would the old interests and occupations come to the fore again?

Peter settled it, 'I go a-fishing' to which six of the others added, 'We also go with thee.' Nothing greatly wrong with what they wanted to do, but that was not the purpose of their being there; they were there to wait. The words, 'I go a-fishing' indicate a return to the old way of life. The words also have a message for others. They seem to say, 'Do what you wish to do, wait if you will, but as for me, "I go a-fishing."' It comes as no surprise, therefore, that having fished all night when conditions were favourable, they caught nothing, whereas, when they fished at the Lord's bidding during the day when conditions were unfavourable, the nets broke because of the haul.

The One who said, 'Follow me and I will make you fishers of men' does not want to hear the words, 'I go a-fishing,' and 'We also go with thee.' They indicate a self-will; the using of a former way of life to make a point. They are the expression of disapproval of the conditions of the moment; more perhaps of irritation than a turning back. Whatever Peter intended, circumstances proved him wrong. He might as well have spent the night in comfort waiting, than to toil all night and catch nothing. 'I go a-fishing' does not always result in catching fish.

*To give light to **them that sit in darkness** and in the shadow of death, to guide our feet into the way of peace.* LUKE 1:79

*T*here is a sombre chill about the words of Zacharias, 'them that sit in darkness', especially when the rest of the statement is added, 'and in the shadow of death.' These words, spoken prophetically as he addressed his son, John Baptist, just after he was born, clearly intimate the condition of the people to whom John would preach; a condition which would also be prevalent when the Lord Himself commenced His public ministry. The people so described were highly favoured. Over many years the grace of God had been made known to them, yet despite that, they were as those who sat in darkness and in the shadow of death.

The words, 'them that sit in darkness' have been a kind of vision to thousands of the Lord's people; a vision which has caused many to rise to the challenge of the eternal needs of men and women estranged from God and living in the darkness of sin. Few have found that the message they carried swept all before them. Most found out that the people who sat in darkness did not see it that way. Indeed, the Saviour met the same attitude. 'We have Abraham to our father' was said to Him in an endeavour to make known to Him that His ministry was quite superfluous and they did not need His offer of mercy. This state of affairs is what makes witnessing for the Lord in many lands so difficult and frustrating. Most of the people who sit in darkness are either not aware of it or do not want to know about its peril.

Happily, the prophecy of Zacharias in Luke 1, from which this meditation is taken has many bright notes, including the lovely statement, 'The dayspring from on high hath visited us.' The One so described was not born when Zacharias prophesied, but as far as he was concerned it was a fact of the past. Whether others believed it or not did not detract from the truth of it, 'The dayspring from on high hath visited us, to give light to them that sit in darkness and in the shadow of death.' Many more may yet get the vision of humanity's peril. Many more will respond to the challenge. May it be as they do, that they will be aware that they carry the tidings of the 'tender mercy of our God.'

For this cause shall a man leave his father and mother, and shall be joined unto his wife, and they two shall be one flesh. EPHESIANS 5:31

There are two words which turn up occasionally. They look alike and sound very similar but there is an essential difference. The words are **introspection** and **introversion**. Introspection carries the meaning of a viewing of the inside; an observing of the processes of one's mind. It is not an unhealthy exercise if it concerns an occasional self-examination; a sort of stock-taking to check how the thinking process is behaving. Introversion is unfortunately more common and concerns the more morbid process of being occupied overmuch with one's inner state and desires. This can be unhealthy and difficult to shake off if it becomes an established condition.

Happily for the Christian there is a better occupation. Paul, writing to the Philippians, sums it up beautifully, 'Think on these things', and he gives a list of Christian graces to consider. From another point of view, the writer to the Hebrews moves on a similar line, 'Looking off unto Jesus, the author and finisher of faith.' Turning the attention away from the inside or even from the influences of problems on the outside and focusing the attention on Christ is a wonderful safeguard.

The words 'For this cause' are an encouragement to consider something very near to the heart of the Lord. It is noted in Scripture as 'a great mystery' but Paul adds quickly, 'I speak concerning Christ and the Church.' The statement in Ephesians 5:32 is introduced by a reference to Genesis 2:24, a natural process, 'For this cause shall a man leave his father and his mother and shall be joined unto his wife.' The man moves out of the sphere where he was subject to headship and he assumes headship on his own account; he and his wife together as one flesh. There is no mystery about that; it was known from the beginning. The great secret being revealed concerned Christ and the Church.

Here then is a tremendous subject for quiet contemplation — Christ and the Church! Think of what that means to the Lord. Think of what it means to God. Take the words which introduce the natural process and apply them to Christ, 'Christ loved the Church — for this cause — and gave Himself for it.' That should be a cure for introversion.

52

And it came to pass, *when the time was come that* He *should be received up,* He *stedfastly set* His *face to go to Jerusalem.* LUKE 9:51

There is an expression in the Greek text which the translators of the A.V. have rendered, 'And it came to pass.' The expression occurs in English in Luke's Gospel nearly fifty times, which is about as much as the other Gospel writers put together.

Since Luke set out to put on record certain things concerning the man Christ Jesus and the effect His life and ministry had on others, the little expression he uses so often *'and it came to pass'* has much to say about life's events. In a general way it seems to suggest that the wheels of life grind steadily on and the things that were ordained by a higher hand came to pass, and nothing could change their course. In the Saviour's life this was totally acceptable. Whatever came to pass in His journey through, He accepted as from the hand of God and He glorified God in every detail. How clearly this comes out is seen in such passages as Luke 9:51, 'And it came to pass when the time was come that He should be received up, He steadfastly set His face to go to Jerusalem.' Or, Luke 17:11,12, 'And it came to pass as He went to Jerusalem, that He passed through the midst of Samaria and Galilee … and there met Him ten men that were lepers.' Or even the last occurrence of the expression at Luke 24:51, 'And it came to pass while He blessed them, He was parted from them, and carried into heaven.' Nothing happened to Him by chance, but as life's events unfolded, He accepted that the things that came to pass were according to the will of God.

Mankind did not recognise the hand of God in the affairs of life, but that did not influence God's purposes. Luke 2:1 makes that very clear, 'And it came to pass in those days, that there went out a decree from Caesar Augustus, that all the world should be taxed.' That had to happen, and it came to pass that the Old Testament scriptures were fulfilled. For the believer, however, there is a happier note, as for instance, Luke 24:4, 'And it came to pass as they were perplexed thereabout, behold two men stood by them in white apparel,' and they heard the message, 'He is not here, He is risen.' And again, at Luke 24:15, 'And it came to pass as they communed together … Jesus Himself drew near.' The events of life are no doubt bewildering, indeed perplexing, but the attitude of the Saviour in the tangles of life which surrounded Him, is the key to them all. Whatever came to pass in His life, He accepted as from the hand of God. Difficult to accept, but is there another way?

'Whatever came to pass in His life,
He accepted as from the hand of God.'

And He began again to teach by the sea side: and there was gathered unto Him a great multitude, so that He entered into a ship, and sat in the sea; and the whole multitude was by the sea on the land. MARK 4:1

The words 'And He began again' are an introduction to another season of service in the working life of Jesus Christ, the Son of God. The writer, Mark, differs from the other Gospel writers in the way he puts his materials together. He, more than the others, lists events as they happened and so the readers of his Gospel can draw from the details what sort of events were handled in a typical day in the life of the Lord. One notable day is found in Mark 1, from verse 21 to verse 34, which is followed by the beginning of the next day, 'And in the morning, rising up a great while before day, He went out, and departed into a solitary place and there prayed.'

The striking thing about the days or seasons of service in the Lord's life is that each one was finished to the glory of God…and He began again! There was no question in the life of this indefatigible servant of God of thinking that He had done enough and it was time for someone else to carry on the work. From early morning until late at night He laboured, and rising early in the following morning, and after prayer, He began again.

Christian service is not an easy path. There may be times when life's events pass smoothly, but inevitably the sorrows and the disappointments, the worries and the frustrations, and even the failures, come. In times like these we need encouragement. The tendency is there to lie back, or even to give up. Where better to look when things begin to collapse than to the Lord? What better example could there be than His when weariness upsets the equilibrium and the tired spirit cries out, 'enough!'? Mark has a touch of comfort and encouragement, 'And He began again to teach by the seaside and there was gathered unto Him a great multitude.' How often that happened in the Saviour's life. If He had listened to the advice of His disciples, 'send them away' how much would have been lost. But not this man. Whatever happened in His life, He accepted it as from the hand of God, He completed it…and He began again. Far better to leave yesterday's sacrifices as ashes under the altar and for today's service for the Master…begin again!

And Jesus said, **Make the men sit down**. Now there was much grass in the place. So the men sat down, in number about five thousand. JOHN 6:10

*T*he words 'Make the men recline' were the words of the Lord at the feeding of the 5,000, a miracle which is included in all four Gospels. The command was given before the five barley loaves and the two small fishes were multiplied. It was a test of faith. With much doubt in their hearts and not a little sarcasm in their voices, the disciples looked upon the smallness of the resources and the vastness of the problem. To them there was no way that one could be covered by the other.

The conditions were favourable. John in his Gospel notes that there was much grass in that place, and Mark in his Gospel notes that the grass was green. Matthew notes that there was grass but does not remark on the quantity or the quality; and Luke makes no mention of grass at all. As far as he was concerned, the important point was the reclining at ease before being fed full at the hand of the Lord. Such is life. Some see quality, others see quantity. Some barely see anything and others miss it altogether. But put together the various appreciations make up very favourable conditions; there may be much green grass in a place.

Where the Lord works is His prerogative. His servants often baulk at the lack of this or the lack of that in the place where they are called to serve. If only there was grass, or even, if only the grass was green, how different it would be. Perhaps another look at the conditions, which yesterday were barren, would reveal that there is both quantity and quality, colour and abundance when the next step of faith is taken. When that is the case, the command of the Lord, 'Make the men recline' is just an indication that He is about to bless. Preparing the ground in faith is an invitation to the Lord to come in, and when He does, even if resources are small, little is much if the Lord is in it.

How many times the lack of faith has been faced with a similar situation to the sequel to the feeding of the 5,000; twelve baskets filled with the fragments that remained. One for each of the disciples who said at the commencement when the five barley loaves and two fishes were produced, 'And what is that amongst so many.'

*Whether therefore ye eat, or drink, or whatsoever ye do, **do all to the glory of God.*** 1 Corinthians 10:31

*I*t is a very common practice in many branches of society for organisations to adopt mottoes in support of their activities. Some of these mottoes set very high standards, such as the one in business life which claims, 'We always seek to please.'

Christian circles are not above adopting mottoes, some taking passages from the scriptures, and others using trite sayings, such as, 'All the Word of God for all the people of God.' This may be very commendable in some ways, considering that a motto in English is said to be a short expression of a guiding principle, or a phrase which is indicative of the character of a person, or a family, or an organisation. But Christians should not really be dependent upon mottoes to enhance their testimony, however admirable the motto might be, even the statement at the head of this meditation from 1 Corinthians 10:31, which is described by a well-known commentator as the supreme motto of Christian life. They should rather seek to become familiar with all the Word of God, rather than taking refuge behind a motto which proclaims it.

The problem about taking mottoes from the Bible is that they are wrested from their context, and the real force of the words in Holy Scripture is lost. The statement, therefore, 'Do all to the Glory of God,' while it means what it says, 'All to the Glory of God,' a very demanding standard, is best appreciated when considered in the context of 1 Corinthians 10, because that is where the Holy Spirit chose to put it.

In a complex world of different cultures, eating habits, and ways of life, the Christian has a difficult task, keeping the conscience clear, and at the same time making sure that the consciences of others are free from offence. Paul describes this world of people in 1 Corinthians 10 as he seeks to map out a sure footing in what is really the swamp of daily living. Christians can sink in this social quagmire, and it is essential, therefore, to keep in mind the quotation twice given in 1 Corinthians 10, 'The earth is the Lord's and the fulness thereof.' It is not a question of exercising one's personal whims or preferences, it is one of pleasing God and thereby helping man. What to eat and what to drink, what to buy and what not to buy, may impose difficulties when they are produced by others in the course of social contact, or sold in the market, but if the earth is the Lord's and the fulness thereof, ordinary things, even unpleasant things can become noble activities when they are covered by the injunction, 'Do all to the glory of God.' The guiding principle of life must ever and always be, 'THE GLORY OF GOD.'

'The earth is the Lord's and the fulness thereof.'

Learn of Me.   MATTHEW 11:29

*I*t is not so many generations back since entrants into most trades were apprenticed to masters. For several years of training they lived and worked and learned the skills of whatever trade with seasoned tradesmen. If the tutor was sound and had the good of his pupil at heart, the apprentice had every chance of being able to reproduce the skills of his master. But not every tradesman was sound and patient and not every apprentice was teachable and respectful.

How different in the Christian sphere. The Lord is the finest of teachers and it was He who gave out the invitation, 'Learn of Me.' This of course was not an invitation to learn about Him; this could be done at college or from books without ever coming under His influence. It is more the practice of the apprentice of old, living and working long hours every day with the master and, being in his company, hear him say, 'Watch the way I do things' and then being encouraged, 'Now do it the way I have done it.'

The record of the four Gospels is certainly about the things that Jesus began, both to do and teach. What He taught did not say much about His own graces. These were reflected in the way He lived and i the way He spoke. He certainly claimed to be meek and lowly in heart, but in doing so He was merely stating facts. He was stating, in as many words, a well-known principle of humility, 'The man who has no opinion of himself can never be hurt if others do not acknowledge him, and he who is without expectation cannot fret if nothing comes to him.' The Saviour in being meek and lowly was above all others, and opinions about Himself did not move or affect Him.

If life is lived according to certain tenets, call them rules and regulations, this is not Christian living. The teachings of Holy Scripture may be parameters, like river banks to guide the flow, but Christian life is lived from the inside out, certainly not the other way round. When the Saviour said 'Learn of Me' He added, 'and ye shall find rest unto your souls.' Did He mean that one

could learn a little about Him and then lie back, or did He mean that in the learning process, living with Him throughout life, one would slowly grow into maturity of purpose and consequently, satisfaction and peace? Although He said 'Learn of Me' the goal is never reached down here, living and learning are life-long, but that kind of living is life indeed.

Stand in awe, *and sin not: commune with your own heart upon your bed, and be still. Selah.* PSALMS 4:4

*T*his short meditation comes from Psalm 4. It is known as the evening hymn, just as Psalm 3 is known as the morning hymn. Both Psalms were written by David when he fled from his son, Absolam, and the sense of deliverance from peril is very marked, as for example the words of Psalm 4:1, 'Thou hast enlarged me when I was in distress.'

The opening words of Psalm 4:4 are, 'Stand in awe and sin not.' In Ephesians 4:26 (and in the Septuagint), these words are given as, 'Be ye angry and sin not' and some good authorities give the phrase as simply, 'Tremble and sin not.' All of these variations are complementary and make an interesting and challenging meditation, especially as the Psalmist notes in the same verse, 'Commune with your own heart upon your bed and be still.' Being an evening hymn, the night is noted as the time for quiet reflection: it is then that things take on a different perspective; during the day they may be coloured.

Paul's view of Psalm 4:4 gives the christian attitude to provocation. Anger not soon settled soon results in broken communion and an unsettled condition upon which the devil can act with advantage. Wrath was not to be nursed; revenge was to form no part of the responses of the new man.

The Psalmist's view may be slightly different. 'Stand in awe and sin not' considers the reverence due to Jehovah. Such was the reverence given to the name, Jews trembled to use it, and so in everyday conversation, and even in their devotions, the Jews used the name Adonai (Lord).

Putting all these thoughts together, standing in reverential awe of God; sinning not; letting not the sun go down on wrath; giving no place to the devil, and meditating quietly in the night seasons, must surely result in the benefit of Psalm 4:8, 'I will both lay me down in peace and sleep, for Thou, Lord, only makest me to dwell in safety.' Perhaps a better rendering of the latter half of this verse would be, 'For Thou, Jehovah, alone makest me to dwell in safety.' Others may fail, but God is always sufficient for all things. In view of that, the attitude of the Psalmist is certainly understandable, 'Stand in awe and sin not.'

'I will both lay me down
in peace and sleep, for
Thou, Lord, only
makest me to dwell
in safety.'

*It is of the Lord's mercies that we are not consumed, because **His compassions fail not**.* LAMENTATIONS 3:22

he little book which contains the lamentations of Jeremiah is one of the most touching in the Old Testament. True to its title, it unfolds the Prophet's lament in the presence of the Lord because of what had befallen Jerusalem and her people. Since Jeremiah's voice had been heard on many occasions giving warnings about the consequences of departure from God it would have been reasonable to expect him to say, 'I told you so' when the blow fell. But out of a true heart, instead of overmuch reproach and rebuke for not heeding his prophetic utterances, he pleaded for a people who were, as has been said, 'as the apple of Jehovah's eye.'

The promise, 'His compassions fail not' comes from Lamentations 3:22. This chapter of sixty-six verses is very remarkable. Each of the first three verses begins with the first letter of the Hebrew alphabet. The next three verses begin with the second letter of the alphabet, and so on until three occurrences of the twenty-two letters of the Hebrew alphabet cover sixty-six verses. Many parts of the Old Testament have an alphabetical arrangement: it was a method of making sure that the burden of what was being written had full coverage as far as language was concerned; no letter of the alphabet being missed out.

The third chapter, or the third poem of Lamentations must have been very special since every letter has a threefold mention. This is not hard to find in the centre of the chapter where there are several blocks of three verses dealing with the mercies of the Lord, and verse 22 is the first one,

> 'It is of the Lord's mercies that we are not consumed,
> because His compassions fail not.'

The next verse expands the thought,

> 'They are new every morning
> great is Thy faithfulness.'

And the third verse rounds it off,

> '"The Lord is my portion" saith my soul,
> "therefore will I hope in Him."'

There ought never to be any thought that there is change with God. Things around may change. Some may wish to join Elijah under the Juniper tree because of change, but one thing is certain, and all can hold on to it, 'His compassions fail not, they are new every morning.'

'The Lord is my portion" saith my soul,
"therefore will I hope in Him.'

*And God said unto Jacob, **Arise, go up to Beth-el**, and dwell there: and make there an altar unto God, that appeared unto thee when thou fleddest from the face of Esau thy brother.* GENESIS 35:1

There is a very striking word of direction at the beginning of Genesis 35. It was an unmistakeable command with a message as applicable today as it was when given thousands of years ago.

The significance of the command is connected with a decision made by Jacob and recorded at the close of Genesis 33 where it is stated that he built a house at Succoth and bought a parcel of ground in Shechem. From the consideration of the events before and after the purchase it becomes obvious that Jacob had made a dreadful mistake. There was no word of direction from above to cause him to settle down socially, and although he built an altar there and gave it a high-sounding name, the heavens were silent and tragic events followed, as noted in Genesis 34.

The plain word of God, 'Arise, go up to Bethel' must have brought back vivid memories of the place where he had heard the voice of God and where he had vowed his vow. Twenty years were to pass before he would hear that voice again, directing him back to that hallowed spot, and it came to him when he had settled in the wrong place. This time Jacob did not wrestle with a divine stranger as at Peniel, neither did he experience again the magnificent sight of the angelic host at Mahanaim. It was just the plain word of God he heard, and he acted immediately. The idols, the baubles, the vanities with all their worldly and religious associations which his household had collected over many years were hidden under an oak tree, and Jacob set off, as directed, to Bethel.

Jacob's response to the command was magnificent. The God who had spoken to him twenty years before was speaking to him again. He was being given the chance to return and he welcomed it gratefully. Some may consider that since Jacob was such a schemer, he did not deserve such favour, but then, who does? Looking back over life, be it over many years or few, will only confirm that grace from above, no matter upon whom it falls, is unmerited.

Here then is a command. Is it applicable? Is there a sphere of service beckoning? Houses and estates as at Shechem may be socially acceptable but they should not shut out the possibility of hearing a word of direction, such as the one given to Jacob, with all its implications, 'Arise, go up to Bethel!'

*And beside this, giving all diligence, **add to your faith** virtue; and to virtue knowledge; And to knowledge temperance; and to temperance patience; and to patience godliness; And to godliness brotherly kindness; and to brotherly kindness charity.* 2 PETER 1:5–7

The exhortation, 'add to your faith' is placed by the apostle Peter at the head of a list of virtues in 2 Peter 1:5–7. At first reading it would seem that Peter had in his mind a situation in which virtue was added to virtue like building blocks being placed one on top of another. Such a thought would stem from the rather inadequate translation in the Authorised Version resulting in the little word 'add'.

The word Peter used contains the thought of a rich supply, an abundance; a liberality which provides far more than is barely necessary. So, an expanded rendering of the phrase quoted might read, 'in your faith, lavishly supply virtue, and in your virtue, lavishly supply knowledge…' Indeed, there is a rendering which makes the phrase one of surpassing interest; it suggests, 'having in your faith', that is, all the virtues are there potentially. Given time and under the influence of the Holy Spirit, they will all come out in generous supply.

Peter is not looking at the christian life as one of chronic inertia, punctuated at long intervals by spasms of activity; he is pressing for all diligence to be applied to a service which will be effective for God and to man. It is wrong to lie back as if the ultimate has been reached; the generosity of God does not absolve a Christian from effort, and faith is never held out to be an exemption from works.

The exhortation calls for a productive life resulting from the fact that God has given to His own all things that pertain to life and godliness. For this very reason, Peter appeals for all diligence to supply from faith, moral excellence, knowledge, self-control, endurance, godliness, brotherly-kindness, love. And then, having made the appeal, he promises, 'for if these things be in you and abound you shall neither be idle nor unfruitful in the knowledge of our Lord Jesus Christ'.

*And not **holding the Head**, from which all the body by the joints and bands having nourishment ministered, and knit together, increaseth with the increase of God.* COLOSSIANS 2:19

There is a tremendous reservoir of grace and energy at the right hand of God in the person of Christ. Paul in many passages of the New Testament scriptures labours to make Christians aware that the benefits are there for them to draw upon, as if sometimes said in the ordinary affairs of life, 'they are there for the asking'.

So in Colossians 2, the apostle makes known how the Head in Heaven imparts His grace and power. Believers are in the body which is knit together in a unity of God's making. All its parts are functional, like joints and ligaments, and through them a lavish supply from the Head is ministered. Whatever is needed percolates down from the Head through the members and not one is missed. As in the human body, the impulses from the brain can reach down to activate any part, right to the extremities.

The metaphor is not hypothetical. It illustrates a practical situation. Each member has a living connection with the Head, and as the body as a whole increases, so each member shares in the body's progress. It is a wonderful contemplation that men and women who are in touch with the Head can come out in all the sensibilities of Christ. He it is who gives directions to the members, hence the appeal of Paul to hold the Head.

A loose connection with the risen Christ involves a limited progress in the Christian life and results in a serious loss for the members. Every believer who lets go the Head causes a blocked channel of communication, a severing of a channel of spiritual life, which causes a circumvention by the Head to by-pass the blockage that other members of the body might not suffer. There is no such thing contemplated in the present dispensation as a believer going in for a monastic way of life; each is vitally necessary for the life of the body. In this connection, the classical example in the New Testament of a believer holding the Head is Phoebe, who is mentioned in Romans 16 as a servant of the church, and a succourer of many. She was indeed an artery in the body, and the members benefited from her function, even the apostle who wrote to the Colossians and exhorted them to hold the Head fast.

The spiritual state

is reached by diligence

in the word of God and in prayer.

> *Brethren, if a man be overtaken in a fault, **ye which are spiritual**, restore such an one in the spirit of meekness; considering thyself, lest thou also be tempted.* GALATIANS 6:1

*S*pirituality is a quality in Christians which is difficult to define. It is nevertheless very real and without it there can be no prosperity in the Lord. The word 'spiritual' is a word of rich positive substance, yet that substance remains to many, a mysterious elusive quality.

Understandably, spirituality is the cherished portion of most believers at all times and the personal knowledge that one is considered to be a spiritual brother or a spiritual sister is most comforting. It means that others have recognised something of the characteristic evidences of the presence and outworking of the Holy Spirit. Although, however much that may be so in the appreciation of men and women, the real test is how one is considered by the Lord.

Spirituality is not a goal to be prized; an honour to be gained once and for all. It is a quality which grows in a believer. It shines out in a myriad of ways; the undeniable tokens of the Holy Spirit's residence and controlling influence in the life. It is not a mysterious quality reserved exclusively for a certain few to be manifested on special public occasions: rather is it the common heritage of every child of God, but only enjoyed and demonstrated in the measure that the Holy Spirit's influence is allowed to hold sway.

It is generally the case amongst believers that there is a reasonable freedom in matters pertaining to life, but a stiffness in relation to spiritual things. Most people manifest an ease of movement which reflects an intimate knowledge of the functions of daily life, but when spiritual things are introduced the aptitude and familiarity are not so evident. The uneasiness indicates that they are not so accustomed to movement in spiritual spheres and to speaking of the things of God.

In early times there was a class which our Lord could count upon in His assemblies. Paul knew of their existence and he addressed them, calling them 'Ye which are spiritual' (Gal 6:1). But some may be disposed to ask, 'Who amongst the saints at Galatia would lay claim to be amongst the spiritual?' Perhaps what one notable servant has written will answer the question. 'The spiritual state is reached by diligence in the word of God and in prayer; it is maintained by obedience and self-judgement. Such as are led by the Spirit are "spiritual".' There must have been some at Galatia, or Paul's letter would have been returned, marked, 'Not known'.

*Wherefore, my beloved, as ye have always obeyed, not as in my presence only, but now much more in my absence, **work out your own salvation** with fear and trembling.* PHILIPPIANS 2:12

*T*he exhortation from Paul to the Philippians of 'work out your own salvation' is not what it appears to be at first sight. It is not a reference to the initial work of God in the soul when a person turns to God in faith; it refers rather to the other end of the work, salvation being brought through to the goal.

Some consider Paul's exhortation to be an appeal to the assembly at Philippi to work out its own salvation. That may be so, but there is another aspect which should not be overlooked; the appeal to individuals. The word used by Paul, rendered 'work out', is one which is recognised as an intensive compound, that is, by reason of its prefix it is charged with an intensified meaning. The force of the word will therefore be that the work begun by God in a believer must be earnestly worked at in the life of the Christian until life itself is finished. To lose impetus, to stop halfway would be contrary to the meaning of the word altogether. The christian life is not an initial spasm followed by chronic inertia, but a working out of what God has worked in.

When God carries out a work of salvation in a person, in one way that work is finished. In the work of salvation the initial thrust of power is of God. The continuing supply of energy is also of God, but the participation of the believer in the work is not just a passive observance; it is an active contribution. Divine working and human involvement are not incompatible.

In the present age of grace God is giving an opportunity to each believer to work with Him in developing a life, just one life (one's own life), to bring it through to final salvation. This is an inestimable privilege. The ultimate challenge is to bring life and character through and into the presence of God without shame. What is acquired on the way through is merely baggage which, as has often been said, must be left at the toll-bar of God: there is no place for it on the other side.

Admittedly, life will have many trials, indeed may at times be quite horrendous to some, but come what may, the exhortation remains the same, 'Work out your own salvation in fear and trembling'.

*And the Lord said unto him, Arise, and go into the street which is called Straight, and inquire in the house of Judas for one called Saul, of Tarsus: for, **behold, he prayeth.***

ACTS 9:11

*W*hen Elijah was sent to Zarephath to be sustained by a widow woman, he did not expect to find her gathering two sticks to prepare the last meal for herself and her son before they died. However, in the good of the experience of being sustained by the brook Cherith, what the prophet found at Zarephath was not beyond the God he had already proved and he had the answer.

Peter and John were also given strange directions when they were sent into Jerusalem to find the place where the Lord would celebrate the Passover with His disciples. They were to look for a man carrying a pitcher of water; a very unusual sight as only women carried pitchers of water in these parts. Rebekah at the well and the woman of Samaria at Sychar were evidences of the normal way of life. But whatever shortcomings marked Peter and John, doubting was not one of them, so they went into the city as instructed and they found the man with the pitcher of water, just as the Lord had said.

If the commands given to Elijah and Peter and John tested their faith, the instructions given to Ananias (Acts 9) were a challenge to all that he believed. In the city of Damascus, in the street called 'straight', in the house of Judas was the persecutor of the church, but he would not be making out a list of those who were to be cast into prison, he would be engaged in another occupation — 'behold he prayeth!' In his blindness he would be waiting for the promise of the Lord to be fulfilled by the man whose name he knew but he would not expect that the first word he would hear would be 'brother'. This is the first time the word is used in the Acts of the Apostles and it was used to calm the fears and bring the blessing to the man whose persecuting days were over.

Directions to go here or to go there are not given to God's servants today by the spoken word. There is really no need for direct communication. The Word of God, the turn of circumstances, the apparent need, all combine to indicate the way forward. Widow women, men carrying pitchers of water, persecutors of the church and many other seemingly adverse signs may cause hesitation, but what is at the end of the road? Perhaps a special vessel for the Lord awaiting the touch of the hand and the mention of 'brother'. That vessel might just be engaged as Saul of Tarsus was, 'behold he prayeth!'

73

*That ye might walk worthy of the Lord unto all pleasing, **being fruitful** in every good work, and increasing in the knowledge of God.* Colossians 1:10

The exhortation from Paul to the Colossians (1:10) about being fruitful in the service of God is really part of a prayer for them. It has been said about this short prayer that it teaches more about prayer's request in essence than almost any other passage in the New Testament.

The prayer of Colossians 1 was a result of a report that had come, about the proof of the gospel working in the lives of the Colossians. The report had the effect upon the apostle and his companions of giving them something definite to pray about and so they made two requests. They asked first of all for discernment of God's will, and then they asked for the power to perform it. What Paul requested from God was that the Colossians might fully understand the great truths of Christianity and be given the power to apply them to daily living. In the wisdom of God, this is His order, and it is pointless to go against it by seeking to do great exploits for God before obtaining a grounding in the truth.

Fruit bearing is not produced by making fruit an object; it is the outcome of having Christ as the object, of thinking of Him, of being occupied with Him. The significance of fruit may be said to be the expression of Christ in the believer; the reproduction of Christ in His people. If service and work were fruit, fruit-bearing would be limited to those who possessed the ability and opportunities to serve. If, however, fruit is the expression of the character of Christ, then it becomes a possibility, as well as a privilege, for every believer to bear fruit for God.

In the prayer, fruit-bearing is linked to walk and every good work. Walk has to do with the believer's passage through this world, and that should be consistent with the character of Christ. Good works are not in themselves fruit for God. The natural man can perform good works but they are not registered in heaven as fruit. Good works, performed by the believer, if done as an outcome of having been occupied with Christ, will have the assured result; they will be classed as fruit, and the believer will be recognised (at least by heaven) as 'being fruitful'.

Fruit-bearing is linked to walk

and every good work.

Walk has to do with the believer's passage

through this world.

Salute Tryphena and Tryphosa, *who labour in the Lord.* Romans 16:12

Of the twenty-eight people mentioned in the list of Christians at Rome to whom Paul sent greetings, eight of them were women. Two of them are not named; one being referred to as the mother of Rufus and the other as the sister of Nereus. Of the remaining six, Priscilla was the wife of Aquila and Junias was probably the wife of Andronicus. This leaves Mary, Tryphena and Tryphosa, and Persis, four women about whom little is known, but from the few words recorded against their names, were on the mind of Paul as being outstandingly faithful in the work at Rome.

Since Paul sent his respects to believing households, brethren, and saints, taking care not to exclude any in his greetings, the mention of the four women by name makes them stand out a little from the others. Although little is known about them, in the brief comments associated with each one there is enough to cause some heart-searching amongst those who may be exercised to consider the apostle's comments.

Mary and Persis may be classed together as having laboured in the past. The mood and tense of the verb used to describe their toil indicates that the work they had done was like the ashes under the altar — evidence of the sacrifices they had made. If, however, these two women were on the retired list as far as physical labour was concerned, they were not out of mind in the reckoning of Paul; he had not forgotten; in their day they had toiled for the Lord.

The remaining two, Tryphena and Tryphosa, were probably sisters. The word used by Paul to describe their labour is the same as the one he dictated about Mary and Persis, but with this difference, it was a present participle, as if to say, 'Give my respects to Tryphena and Tryphosa who are toiling hard at this moment in the work of the Lord'. There is no suggestion that these two women were on the retired list. Their names might suggest that they were Dainty and Delicate, but the labour they were expending belied the impression conveyed in what they were called.

As a voice from the past it is challenging to consider that in each successive generation there are those whose sacrifices call for recognition and to them Paul's greeting keeps going out, 'Salute Tryphena and Tryphosa — be encouraged, your present labours are not forgotten'.

*And after he had seen the vision, immediately we endeavoured to go into Macedonia, **assuredly gathering** that the Lord had called us for to preach the gospel unto them.* Acts 16:10

---

*T*he way forward in life is sometimes difficult to ascertain, and because of the apparent lack of guidance, bewilderment often sets in. It is heartening, however, to recognise that servants of God in apostolic times had to deal with the same problem also, and Acts 16 gives a classical example.

The two words 'assuredly gathering' represent one word in the original scripture, and it means to unite, to knit together, or to cause to come together. The way forward for Paul as noted in Acts 16 was affected by certain circumstances but when he knit them together in his mind the path became clear.

The first circumstance was closed doors. Paul had determined to go to Asia but the door closed. He then decided to go to Bithynia but the door closed again. The Holy Spirit made it perfectly clear that he was not to go to either of these areas. How the Holy Spirit communicated the message to Paul is of little consequence, the word of direction was clear enough to the apostle and he had no doubts about the source.

The second circumstance was a report from Macedonia that help was needed. Before the doors to Asia and Bithynia had closed Macedonia was not on the apostle's mind, but here was an indication that another door was opening.

The third circumstance was the place where Paul and his companions were when the report came. They were in Troas, a coastal town just a short sail from Macedonia. They had not intended to be there but when the doors to the north and the east closed, the door to the west opened and they happened to be in the place where a passage by ship was a simple matter, and a straight course brought them to the other side.

'Assuredly gathering' is not laid down as the formula for determining the way forward in life, but the exercise of uniting circumstances such as closed doors and opened doors, the voice of the Spirit from the word of God and being in the right place at the right time is a good one. There is no need to cry to God for a fresh revelation when the indicators are all around just waiting to be assuredly gathered.

There is no need to cry to God for a fresh
revelation when the indicators are all around
just waiting to be assuredly gathered.

Esteeming the reproach of Christ greater riches than the treasures in Egypt:
*for **he had respect** unto the recompence of the reward.* Hebrews 11:26

The three words, 'he had respect' represent one word from the pen of the writer to the Hebrews, and it describes the stance taken by Moses in relation to certain things. It is the only occurrence of the word in the New Testament and that perhaps gives some extra significance to its use.

The expression is found in Hebrews 11:26 and it describes the kind of look adopted by Moses in his consideration of the reward. It was one of wonder; it was a looking away from something to take in something far better. The treasures of Egypt were real, they were substantial and they were there for the enjoyment of Moses if he had cared to make use of them. Some would consider that his choice was totally inexplicable, but as far as he was concerned, he deemed the reproach to be of greater value than the treasures at his disposal and so he looked away. What he looked away from was real, there was little doubt about that, but what he looked away to was no less real. Others could not see it and even if they had looked intently it would have escaped their notice for they had no respect for the reward.

There are many words in the New Testament which are used to describe looking, such as looking round, looking for, looking after, looking diligently, but the one which describes the look of Moses has something special about it. It describes the conscious deliberation of putting the things of the world in their proper place, even to the point of considering the good things as reproach, and then looking away with wonder and amazement to contemplate something far better.

There are two horizons before the Christian. The sorrowful fact is that some seldom lift their eyes above the horizons of earth: they are earthbound, and although the horizons of heaven beckon them, they see nothing on which to fix their gaze. Moses was different; his earnest gaze was fixed on the heavenly horizon, and to the eye of faith that was not far distant. He looked away and he kept looking because what he looked at never lost its substance — he had respect unto the recompense of the reward.

*And Esau said, **I have enough**, my brother; keep that thou hast unto thyself. And Jacob said, Nay, I pray thee, if now I have found grace in thy sight, then receive my present at my hand: for therefore I have seen thy face, as though I had seen the face of God, and thou wast pleased with me. Take, I pray thee, my blessing that is brought to thee; because God hath dealt graciously with me, and because **I have enough**. And he urged him, and he took it.* Genesis 33:9–11

---

he context for this short meditation is Genesis 33:9–11, where the expression 'I have enough' occurs twice, once as stated by Esau to Jacob and once in Jacob's reply to Esau. According to the Authorised Version, both brothers claim, as far as this world's goods are concerned, 'I have enough'. At first sight then, Esau, the carnal man, and Jacob, the spiritual man (with all his shortcomings), both claim to be totally satisfied; both have enough.

There are not many in the world who will readily say, 'I have enough'. In fact, there is a word in the New Testament which occurs again and again, *pleonexia*, the sin of greed. It has been described as 'the accursed love of possessing, the aiming always at getting more'.

Regarding Esau and Jacob, a closer look at what they claimed reveals a difference. The Hebrew, and the Greek version of the Hebrew Scriptures, both record that the two men used different words. Esau really stated, 'I have much' and Jacob replied, 'I have all', or as the J.N.D. version has it, 'I have everything'. This then leaves room for Esau to add to his possessions. Although he did not want anything from Jacob, there was always scope for adding more, if the desire and the occasion arose. If Jacob meant what he said, then he was totally satisfied. When a person arrives at the point of saying 'I have everything', the sin of greed has lost its appeal; it has no longer any force.

Although Jacob claimed to have everything (according to the J.N.D. version), there is something softer and more dignified about the phrase used in the Authorised Version, 'I have enough'. To deal with the passage properly it would not be right to change the meaning of what Esau said and leave Jacob's reply unchanged. However, if Jacob said 'I have all' that must mean 'I have enough', and in this world, the world of *pleonexia*, it is encouraging to think that there are still many who are content with what they have. Perhaps the hymnwriter expressed the correct attitude for this age when he wrote, 'I have Christ, what want I more?'

*But we have this treasure in earthen vessels, that **the excellency of the power** may be of God, and not of us.* 2 Corinthians 4:7

The very wonderful expression 'the excellency of the power' is found in 2 Corinthians 4:7. At first reading it would seem to suggest that it is something enjoyed by the apostle and his fellow-workers, the experience of a select few to know and demonstrate the excellency of the power of God.

The context in which the expression occurs does not support the view that it is the exclusive possession of some who have attained to a higher experience; it points rather in the opposite direction. It is a reminder that the condition God works best with is weakness, nothingness, even fearfulness, so that the excellency of the power might be of God and not in human strength.

In 2 Corinthians 4:7 there is a tremendous contrast between 'the treasure' and 'the earthen vessel'. The two expressions cover the excellency of the message and the frailty of the messenger. In a normal setting a treasure is contained in a vessel suited to the dignity and value of the treasure. But in the wisdom of God, the gospel of God has been placed in what would appear to be the most unsuitable container. It seems so unlikely that something so precious, a treasure of inestimable value should be exposed to the frailty of a perishable jar. But therein lies the wisdom of God; the treasure of the gospel has been placed in an object from the potter's hand, frail and mortal.

How wrong it would be to try and make the vessel of greater value than the treasure. This should never be, but unfortunately there are many who act as if it were so. Attention is drawn to the vessel but the treasure, the gospel of the grace of God, is given a secondary place. In that situation there can be no demonstration of the excellency of the power of God.

It is worthy of notice that the verse does not refer to the power of God but to the excellency of the power of God. This is another example of Paul's use of the superlative to describe things which he thinks human language cannot cover adequately. The reference to the excellency of the power is Paul's way of lifting the power on to another plane, a level far above that on which human power operates. Those who know something of this in their lives are those who serve God in the consciousness of being only what they are — earthen vessels!

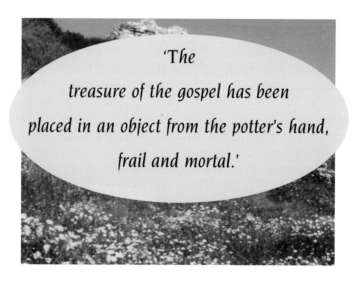

'The treasure of the gospel has been placed in an object from the potter's hand, frail and mortal.'

*Therefore they sought again to take him: but he escaped out of their hand,
And went away again beyond Jordan into the place where John at first
baptized; and there he abode. And many resorted unto him, and said, **John
did no miracle**: but all things that John spake of this man were true.*
JOHN 10:39–41

There are two verses at the end of John 10 which have been a source of encouragement to many since they were written. They concern the retirement of the Lord Jesus to a place beyond Jordan following the opposition that arose against Him as the result of the giving of the shepherd discourse, which is the fourth sermon out of eight recorded in John's Gospel.

The place to which the Lord retired was a spot where John Baptist baptised at the beginning of his ministry. There must have been something special about that spot which was in the mind of the Lord. John was not there; he had been beheaded. The effects of his work were there, however, and although that great servant had gone to his reward, the situation was a classical example of the words associated with Abel, 'he being dead yet speaketh'.

After the opposition of the Jews at the feast of dedication at Jerusalem (and the writer notes that it was winter), it must have been a relief to the Lord's spirit to retire to a spot where many resorted to Him. The inference seems to be that John Baptist's ministry had created a lasting impression on people and they remembered what he had said about the One who would come after him. The result was that the people said, 'John did no miracle, but all things that John spake of this man were true, and many believed on Him there'.

Here is an encouragement for the Lord's servants. It is within the scope of all to create an environment into which the Lord can come. Miracles are of no consequence; what really counts is that all things that are said about the Lord are true, and the Spirit will build on that. It may be that the results will not be seen in one's lifetime. John Baptist did not live to see the fruit of his labours in that spot beyond Jordan but although he did no miracles what he said about the Lord was true and many believed on Him there. As to where the situation is placed in John's Gospel, it is another example of the guidance of the Holy Spirit on the writers of Holy Scripture. Just when the Lord needed it after enduring opposition and just before He had to deal with the death of Lazarus, He had a spot prepared by a servant's ministry. John did no miracle but he certainly left an impression.

'John did no miracle,

but all things that John spake of this man were

true, and many believed on Him there'.

These all died in faith, *not having received the promises, but having seen them afar off, and were persuaded of them, and embraced them, and confessed that they were strangers and pilgrims on the earth.* HEBREWS 11:13

The words 'these all died in faith' are taken from Hebrews 11:13. The reasoning of the writer of the epistle is that the antediluvian saints and the patriarchs never obtained what their faith envisaged. That, however, did not rob them of the joy of their hope. They lived in a material world but they did not conduct their lives according to the practices around them. They were citizens of another realm and they had the ability to embrace its features and live according to its standards.

The Jews, to whom the epistle to the Hebrews was addressed, were encouraged to live for God and be guided by the principles which were held by the worthies of the past. There was always the possibility that they might be called home before the hope of the gospel was realised. That, however, was no reason to alter their way of life. Like those who had gone before, no greater testimony could be recorded than that of Hebrews 11:13, 'These all died in faith'. These five words were quite

sufficient to sum up the life lived for God, and if no other account existed, it would be enough to know that those who died in faith lived according to the same principle.

The psalmist in Psalm 39 expresses how he felt under extreme provocation from the ungodly. As he thought about it he resolved with God's help to be silent. This was not easy for him but it led to better things for while his heart was hot within him his tongue was loosed and he cried to God. He realised his hope was in God and as a stranger and a sojourner he was like his forefathers, cast on God for the future.

There is no good reason for doubting. There is no excuse for deciding to give up. The faithful of the past carried on to the end. They died in faith, not having received the promises, but having seen them afar off, they embraced them and confessed that they were strangers and pilgrims on the earth.

The Lord may come soon. If the day of grace is extended and most, if not all, of the present generation do not experience the upward call of God while living, that should make no difference to the outlook. What characterised the worthies of the past should mark the faithful of the present, so that it can be said, 'These all died in faith'.

*And it came to pass after a while, that **the brook dried up**, because there had been no rain in the land.* 1 KINGS 17:7

---

*E*lijah, the first of the great prophets to Israel, is not introduced in the Bible with a long list of credentials to support him in his office; he just appears, but his message to the wicked king, Ahab, is clear enough. Its source might have been doubted or even denied when he announced it but when the drought came there was no mistaking where the power to put it into practice came from.

The same Lord who gave Elijah the message for Ahab then gave him a word of direction for himself, 'Get thee hence and turn eastward, and hide thyself by the brook Cherith'. Whether that command to hide himself was for his own safety or to let him know that he would be tested by his own ministry, or whatever, Elijah hid himself and was out of the gaze of the public for over three years.

This remarkable man burst out of obscurity, delivered a solemn message for the nation of Israel, and just as quickly as he appeared, was taken out again to the seclusion of the banks of the brook Cherith. It was there that he was fed morning and evening by the ravens and his faith was tried. In some ways there was something idyllic about the quietness of that retreat. He must have been near to God and God must have communed with His servant there, but, be that as it may, he had to watch the level of the water in the brook going down until it reached the point, described simply in Scripture, 'the brook dried up'.

In the service of God it is difficult to accept that faithfulness to His word in public ministry is often followed by a series of trying circumstances. Abraham passed that way, from the triumph over the kings to the horror of great darkness and then on to a fiery furness before the Lord finally made a covenant with him. In Elijah's situation, a widow woman with only a handful of meal and a little oil between her and death was not much improvement on a dried-up brook. But in seclusion and on the verge of having nothing to sustain life, he was still God's chosen vessel with the message for the nation and the power to put it into practice. What was happening apart from the public gaze was providing the ground for the ministry of his Lord nearly 1,000 years further on in time.

To be faced with a situation, 'the brook dried up' may be trying at the time but the long-term effects of the experience will be well worth the sacrifice. Floods of revival may stem from dried-up brooks.

'Floods of revival
may stem
from dried-up brooks.'

*Now for a recompence in the same, (I speak as unto my children,) **be ye also enlarged.*** 2 Corinthians 6:13

_____

The appeal in 2 Corinthians 6:13 for enlargement is not a plea for expansion in material things. An exhortation of that nature would have been lost on the Corinthians. Paul had already acknowledged that they reigned like kings; they were rich; they were wise; they were strong; they were honourable. They did not need any encouragement to expand in natural things; that had become a way of life with them.

The plea of the apostle was for expansion in spiritual things. That appeal came from a worthy servant of God who stated, 'O ye Corinthians, our mouth is opened unto you, our heart is enlarged'. What was said from his opened mouth was a proof of the enlargement of his heart. There were no restrictions with him. He was jealous over the Corinthians with a jealousy of God. He wanted their affections to be reserved in their entirety for the Lord, but there were restrictions. The Corinthians had been side-tracked. They were expanding in the wrong sphere, so much so that the apostle had to state, 'I could not speak unto you as spiritual but as unto carnal, even as unto babes in Christ'.

In Paul's assessment of the Corinthian position he concluded that there was little or no growth in the spiritual realm — the Corinthians were spiritual pygmies. Towards Paul personally there was no evidence of affection to correspond with the enlargement of his heart towards them. Their affections were cramped, confined to a narrow straitened condition of soul, and it all resulted from expansion in the wrong realms. They had not understood that the church was a spiritual organism and that it could only be enlarged by spiritual means. It

had not gripped them that living like kings did not produce spiritual growth. What they needed to manifest was a completely new life-style.

In the context of 2 Corinthians 6, Paul's appeal, 'Be ye also enlarged' is a call for enlargement of affection towards him. It is indicative, however, of the Corinthian malaise — too much of the natural and too little of the spiritual. Perhaps this imbalance is at the root of today's problems as far as christian living is concerned, and if that is so there is a pressing need for an ongoing audit of life. If re-adjustments resulted from the review, there would be little need for Paul's exhortation, 'Be ye also enlarged'.

Yet a little while, and the world seeth me no more; but ye see me: because I live, ye shall live also. At that day ye shall know that I am in the Father, and ye in me, and I in you. John 14:19–20

The wonderful revelation, 'Ye shall live also' is the corollary of the glorious fact, 'Because I live'. There is also an extension to this promise. It was not enough that life in all its fullness for time and eternity was the outcome of the link with His own imperishable life, but there was an added blessing, 'Because I live, ye shall know'.

The deep concern of the disciples as seen in John 14, was the thought of being left to their own resources, but the Lord corrected that outlook by revealing His interest, 'I will not leave you orphans, I will come to you'. He had promised that when He had gone, the Holy Spirit would come. That was not to be understood as meaning that one divine person would be substituted for another. It was intended to convey to the disciples that the coming of the Holy Spirit would secure for them the presence of the Lord for ever.

The men and women of the world have their own pattern of living. The politics and the pleasures reflect what kind of life it is, but it has no link with the statement, 'Because I live, ye shall live also'. The worldling neither lives the new life nor knows the mind of God, but there is a company on earth and those who compromise it live and know. The life which is theirs is eternal in its duration and different in its character. The wonder of the new position is that there are no secrets. Because He lives, the Christian also lives and knows that an intimate link exists between Christ and the Father and between Christ and the believer. Communion with divine persons was not to be a remote possibility, but a vital part of the new life, all the outcome of the work of the Lord as intimated in the momentous statement, 'Because I live, ye shall live also'.

The hymn-writer has written, 'Because He lives, I can face tomorrow'. The sentiment of that is good and true, but it is only an aspect of the basic statement, 'Because I live, ye shall live also'. Once in the good of that, what comes today, tomorrow and the next day are just part of the joy of living the new life.

91

And *after that* went the Levites in to do their service in the tabernacle of the congregation before Aaron, and before his sons: as the LORD had commanded Moses concerning the Levites, so did they unto them.

NUMBERS 8:22

The Levites were a peculiar people among the tribes of Israel. It is true that they were no better than the others, indeed the behaviour of Levi and his brother Simeon came under the severe condemnation of their father, Jacob, in the closing days of his life, 'Instruments of cruelty are in their habitations' (Gen 49:5). When, however, idolatry swept through the camp in the worship of the golden calf, Levi was the only one who responded to the call of Moses, 'Who is on the Lord's side?' That stand taken by Levi was not forgotten by the Lord and so it was that instead of claiming all the firstborn who were spared when the destroying angel passed through the land of Egypt, the tribe of Levi was taken instead.

In the book of Numbers, chapter 8, the account is given of the offering of the tribe of Levi unto the Lord, 'Thus shalt thou separate the Levites from among the children of Israel and the Levites shall be mine, and **after that** shall the Levites go in and do the service of the Tabernacle' (Num 8:14,15).

Following the separation of the Levites, they were then sanctified and purified; they washed their clothes and an offering was made for their cleansing; 'and **after that** shall the Levites go in and do the service of the Tabernacle' (Num 8:22). The two mentions of the words, 'after that' are very significant. They come between two conditions, showing that service for the Lord was not acceptable without the necessary preliminaries. Even after washing, clean clothing had to be worn; there was to be no perpetuation of any aspect of defilement. The break with the past had to be made and **after that** service for the Lord could begin.

In every age service for the Lord should not be considered as a light thing. The necessary preparation of heart and life must be carried out before the Lord and **after that** service can commence. If these two words were weighed up carefully as always being forerunners to service, many pitfalls could be avoided.

*Study to shew thyself approved unto God, a workman that needeth not to be ashamed, **rightly dividing** the word of truth.* 2 TIMOTHY 2:15

*T*he two words 'rightly dividing' are found in 2 Timothy 2:15. They represent one word in the original scriptures and that word only occurs once in the New Testament. The burden on the heart of Paul when he wrote to Timothy was that the young man would **rightly divide** the word of truth as an approved workman of God.

It is possible that Paul had in mind his trade as a tent-maker when he used the word. The pieces of material which had to be cut to make up the tent had to be cut to size, otherwise the finished article would be flawed. Others have suggested that Paul might have had the carpenter in mind cutting his wood, or the ploughman ploughing his furrows, or the stone-mason shaping his stones. Whatever thought was in the mind of the apostle, the importance of handling the word of God in an accurate, unbiased manner weighed heavily upon him.

In the Septuagint, the Greek version of the Old Testament, the Hebrew word 'yashar' is variously interpreted. On two occasions, Proverbs 3:6 and Proverbs 11:5, the word used by Paul in 2 Timothy 2:15 is given as the interpretation of the Hebrew word. In Proverbs 3:6, the verse reads, 'In all thy ways acknowledge Him and He shall **direct** thy paths'. In Proverbs 11:5, the writer gives, 'The righteousness of the perfect shall **direct** his way'. The force of the Hebrew word is 'righteousness' or 'uprightness' which may add another dimension to what Paul wrote to Timothy.

Although it is of absorbing interest to muse upon the different pictures Paul might have had before him when he wrote to Timothy to **rightly divide**, or cut in a straight line the word of truth, it may be nearer the point to consider what Timothy thought as he read the statement. Perhaps he had the Septuagint renderings before him and he judged that Paul meant him to **rightly direct** the word of truth, that is, to **set it forth** in righteousness. Whatever way the word is considered, it most certainly emphasises the importance of handling the word of God with an awesome reverence and godly fear. To convey a wrong meaning, either by design or through carelessness is a very serious matter.

*And I besought thy disciples to cast him out; **and they could not**.*
LUKE 9:40

*I*t must be a very distressing experience to find a lack of power just when it is needed most. This was certainly the case with the disciples when they were confronted by a distraught father and his only child who was demon-possessed. The father begged the disciples to cast the demon out, but the sad comment of Luke 9:40 is, 'and they could not'.

The father of the child was fully entitled to ask the disciples for help. They had just returned from a mission during which they had exercised the power given to them by the Lord to cast out demons and heal diseases. In doing just that they had created an expectancy in the people to enter into the blessings of the kingdom of God and to experience a foretaste of the powers of the age to come (Heb 6:5). But although they had powered their way through the land casting out demons they found themselves in the presence of their Lord having to listen to the despairing cry of a man, 'And they could not'. If Mark's record of events is taken into account they had to face up to the embarrassment of having to ask, 'Why could not we cast him out?'

It is an easy matter to stand off in a detached way and pass censure on the disciples. The Lord made it clear that the reason for their inability to deal with the situation was unbelief. This is further narrowed down to a lack of dependence upon God. Whether that stemmed from carelessness of some kind or another is open to conjecture, but the end result is clear; they were out of touch with the source of power and they suffered the consequences.

There are many lessons to be learned from the inability of the disciples to meet the need of the tormented boy. Very often, like the disciples, and Samson in his day, Christians are not aware that power has departed. Many continue in their everyday life, fully occupied with the mundane things that come across their paths, and are not aware until it is too late that a dearth has crept in and has become an established fact.

'. . . they were out of touch with the source of power and they suffered the consequences.'

Barren experiences could often be avoided if more attention were paid to dependence upon the Lord; there would then be fewer occasions for acknowledging 'and we could not' when it should have been possible to have it said, 'and they did'.

After all this, *when Josiah had prepared the temple, Necho king of Egypt came up to fight against Carchemish by Euphrates: and Josiah went out against him.* 2 Chronicles 35:20

The three words 'after all this' are taken from 2 Chronicles 35:20 mark a turning point in the life of good king Josiah. He came to the throne at the early age of eight years, had serious thoughts of God when he was sixteen years, started to purge the land of evil when he was twenty years and completed the work by the time he was twenty-six.

In addition to all that, he restored the ark to its rightful place in the Holy of Holies and held the passover according as it was written in the book of Moses. Of that passover the Scripture states, 'And there was no passover like to that kept in Israel from the days of Samuel the prophet, neither did all the kings of Israel keep such a passover as Josiah kept' (2 Chron 35:18).

With that wonderful background recorded indelibly in Holy Scripture for succeeding generations to read, the picture is suddenly and abruptly marred by three simple words, 'After all this'. Before proceeding to consider what follows to find the reason for the insertion of the brief statement, a moment's reflection will not be out of place. At the beginning of Josiah's life, before its details are unfolded, the testimony of the Lord is, 'And he did that which was right in the sight of the Lord'. At the end of his life, the brief obituary reads, 'Now the rest of the acts of Josiah and his goodness...behold, they are written in the book of the kings of Israel and Judah (2 Chron 35:26).

Between the words of commendation, 'that which was right' and 'Josiah and his goodness' come the words, 'After all this'. That is, after all the good he had done, he did something foolish, he meddled in the affairs of another, something which he had nothing to do with and he paid the price. Although disguised to avoid being recognised, the archer's arrow found him and he was slain.

The lesson to be learned is surely this. There is enough in the service of God to occupy all His servants without being involved in things that have nothing to do with the testimony. It is a tragedy when lives that have begun well with God are marred by involvement in things that do not have God's approval. The simple words 'After all this' tell many a story in the lives of God's people.

*Ah Lord God! behold, Thou hast made the heaven and the earth by Thy great power and stretched out arm, and **there is nothing too hard for Thee**...* JEREMIAH 32:17

---

he words 'there is nothing too hard for thee' are the opening words of a prayer of Jeremiah's (Jer 32:17). It is a strange prayer, not one of request to get him out of prison but one of report, having completed a transaction given to him by the Lord.

While Jeremiah was in prison he was told he would receive a visit from his cousin, Hanameel, who would offer to sell him a field. This was a strange circumstance as the field was in the land of Benjamin which was overrun by the Chaldeans. No one was buying real estate in those days. The state of the nation under siege made it unlikely that land or property would ever be redeemed. But Jeremiah did not hesitate, he not only bought the field but he tied up all the details legally and then he prayed.

'Ah Lord God...there is nothing too hard for Thee.'

The principle involved was clear. There would come a day when houses, fields and vineyards would be possessed again in the land (Jer 32:15). God would see to that, and Jeremiah was told to show his faith in the promises of God and buy a field, although he might never possess it personally. That did not matter to faith; the title deeds were put in an earthen jar and the field was there in the name of Jeremiah. And so, when the transaction was completed, the prophet prayed and acknowledged, 'There is nothing too hard for thee'.

Mary, the mother of the Lord, asked a question beginning with the word 'How'. The angel Gabriel answered, 'For with God all things are possible'. The disciples asked a question beginning with the word 'Who', and the Lord answered, 'The things which are impossible with men are possible with God'. Today, Christians may not be asked to buy a field in as many words, but they are asked to act in faith to sow the seed, redeem the time, and raise stock for God, although they might never see the result. If there should be a question of 'How' or 'Who', or a doubt about the outcome, Jeremiah's words from the prison should be enough to remove all doubt, 'Ah Lord God...there is nothing too hard for Thee'.

*L*uke's Gospel has many references to the Lord's prayer life. It was after one of His sessions in prayer (Lk 11:1), that one of His disciples made the request, 'Lord, teach us to pray', and this was answered by the giving of the beautiful form of words, beginning 'Our Father, which art in heaven'.

According to Luke's account, this is followed immediately by what is considered by many to be a parable, 'The request of the friend at midnight'. In the parable, the request from outside the house for three loaves of bread is answered from the inside, 'Trouble me not, the door is shut and my children are with me in bed: I cannot rise and give thee'. The appeal for help to provide something for someone on a journey was rejected out of hand. The door was locked and all were settled down for the night, hence the uncompromising reply, 'Trouble me not'.

The Lord then reveals that the bond of friendship was not enough to make the householder rise to meet the urgent need which had arisen. On that ground the answer was curt, 'Trouble me not'. However, because of the importunity of the man who asked, his audacity, his shamelessness, the Lord explained that the householder will not only rise from bed but will rouse himself from any thought of sleep and give his friend as many loaves as he needed.

How different are the ways of God. Could there ever be a time when God answered a midnight cry with the words, 'Trouble Me not'? If audacious shamelessness but not friendship will move men, how will God react to the needs of His own? The lesson in the parable is surely that God is not behind barred doors; He never slumbers and needs to be awakened. Rather is He waiting to answer those who ask, who seek, who knock. Never will He say 'Trouble Me not', but the asker will receive, the seeker will find, and to the one who knocks the door will be opened. He may seem to be tardy in His reply at times but there is wisdom in His withholding. He always knows what time is best to grant. Too soon may answer the asking but remove the need to seek and knock.

*Now the God of hope fill you with all joy and peace in believing, **that ye may abound in hope**, through the power of the Holy Ghost.* ROMANS 15:13

It is very interesting to note that the general teaching of the epistle to the Romans ends at 15:13, and that the last word, as it were, is a short prayer. This prayer is preceded by four wonderful quotations from the Old Testament which all prove the truth of the statement at 15:4, 'For whatsoever things were written aforetime were written for our learning, that we through patience and comfort of the Scriptures might have hope'.

The short closing prayer of 15:13 is addressed to the God of hope, the only occurrence of this description of God in the New Testament. It is a reminder that God is the author and the source of hope. He never despairs and He never fails. He will never give up His own as hopeless, although they may often try His patience. If therefore the God of hope is not rendered powerless by what appear to be hopeless situations, praying Paul's prayer will surely bring results.

If therefore the God of hope is not rendered powerless by what appear to be hopeless situations, praying Paul's prayer will surely bring results.

In the verse, the short prayer is addressed to the God of hope and the desire of the one who prayed was that all he embraced in his prayer should be filled with all joy and peace in believing. But how will all that be made effective? The answer is in the closing words, 'through the power of the Holy Ghost'. The ability to bring about the kind of hope that is part of the Christian faith is not within the power of man; it is the province of the Spirit of God. He knows what is required and He is able to bring it all to pass.

The prayer has two parts. Neither part is within the scope of man's ability to supply because the hope of the Bible is not natural; it is spiritual; it is interwoven in the plans and the will of God. The first part of the prayer calls for a filling with joy and peace which is a reminder that although joy and peace may be there, the level needs to be brought up to full measure. The second half puts the first part into perspective. The fulness of joy and hope must find expression. It seems that Paul's prayer says, 'Let it abound', and if in the power of the Spirit it will be in the correct channels.

'And whatsoever ye do,

do it heartily,

as to the Lord,

and not unto men...'

COLOSSIANS 3:23

> *Now there **stood by the cross** of Jesus His mother, and His mother's sister,*
> *Mary the wife of Cleophas, and Mary Magdalene…and the disciple*
> *standing by, whom He loved…* JOHN 19:25–26

'*N*ow there stood by the cross of Jesus, His mother, and His mother's sister, Mary the wife of Cleophas, and Mary Magdalene…and the disciple standing by, whom He loved.' So writes John in his account of the dark hours in the history of mankind when the Lord was crucified.

Although it is recorded that all forsook Him and fled, and the psalmist wrote prophetically, 'I looked for some to take pity and there was none and for comforters and there was none', there were some who stood around the cross, and some who took their stand at the back of the crowd, as Luke notes, 'And all His acquaintance, and the women that followed Him from Galilee, stood afar off, beholding these things' (Lk 23:49).

In the roll of the book there were prophetic utterances which had to be fulfilled such as, 'He made His grave with the wicked, and was with the rich in His death' (Is 53:9). How would that be accomplished with only a few hours remaining before the sabbath and the Saviour's body still on the cross? Out from obscurity came the secret disciple, the rich man, Joseph of Arimathea, who bought the clean white linen and whose new tomb awaited its first occupant. He was a just man and an honourable counsellor and it was he who found the courage to go to Pilate and beg the body of Jesus. And so, with only a few hours to spare, the Lord was with the rich in His death.

And then there was Nicodemus. Three times he is noted as being that Nicodemus 'who first came to Jesus by night'. But it was not night when he brought a mixture of myrrh and aloes, about a hundred pounds weight, and joined Joseph to perform that last sacred office, according to the manner of the Jews to bury. Where was Nicodemus? Was he standing by the cross or was he standing afar off?

But there was also Mary Magdalene. No need for conjecture as far as she is concerned, for John names her as one of the three, all named Mary, who stood by the cross. The Scripture has something to say about her, just as it identifies Nicodemus as the one who came to the Lord by night. Twice reference is made to Mary Magdalene, out of whom went seven demons. She was the only one named Mary who had experienced that kind of deliverance, and it was not likely that she would forget it quickly. Perhaps that was why she ministered to the Lord of her substance and later stood by the cross.

In every generation followers of the Lord Jesus are given opportunities to take their stand. Some are nowhere to be found when the test comes. Some take up their positions afar off, but happily there are always some who are found 'standing by the cross'.

And he departed, *and began to publish in Decapolis how great things Jesus had done for him: and all men did marvel.* MARK 5:20

*T*here is something about the expression 'and he departed' that catches the eye. It engenders thought. Depending of course on the context in which it is used, it invariably suggests motivation.

The man of the Gadarenes is a classical example of this. Having been told by the Lord to go home to his friends and tell them how great things the Lord had done for him, he did just that. Mark records, 'and he departed, and began to publish abroad in Decapolis how great things that Jesus had done for him, and all men did marvel' (Mk 5:20). If he had stayed where he was amongst the tombstones, there would not have been any declaration of great things.

In the Authorised Version the word is sometimes translated by a cluster of small words, such as 'and he went his way'. An example of this is found in Luke's Gospel where the expression is given to cover the departure of Judas to commune with the chief priests and elders. On occasions the word is translated by the simple expression, 'and they went', as in the case of the disciples who were sent to reserve the upper room. It might have appeared to Peter and John that they were being sent on an unlikely mission. To go to a city and be met by a man bearing a pitcher of water did not appear to be a reception fit for a king, 'but they went' and found it to be as He had said. Many unlikely missions turn out to be successful ones when there is a readiness to go.

Sometimes the word adds the final touch to something done for God. When Joseph of Arimathea stepped out of the shadows to perform the last offices for the Lord, he did them and, as Luke notes, 'he departed'. The special vessel who was reserved by God to fulfil the prophetic word of Isaiah 53:9, 'and He was with the rich in His death' did what was required of him and he departed. He is not mentioned again, but he did his work and went his way. The 'well done, good and faithful servant' could wait until another day.

*Then Jesus answering said unto them, **Go your way, and tell John** what things ye have seen and heard; how that the blind see, the lame walk, the lepers are cleansed, the deaf hear, the dead are raised, to the poor the gospel is preached.* Luke 7:22

Many seasons of ministry which begin with great promise strike patches when things do not seem to be going well. Indeed, like John the Baptist, there may even be serious doubts about whether the Lord knows, or even cares about His servant's plight.

There could hardly have been a more illustrious start to service than that of John the Baptist's. It is not everyone's father who has received a visit from an angel, and it is certain that there are very few who get a mention in the prophetic scriptures in all but name. In addition, to have a mother who was cousin to the woman who would bear the child who was the Messiah, was really a privilege beyond thought.

Despite all that, from a prison cell came the question, 'Art Thou He that should come, or look we for another?' The four walls and the discomfort did not match up with the royal message he had been given to declare, 'Prepare ye the way of the Lord, make his paths straight'. And to make matters worse, his imprisonment was a result of his faithfulness to the law of Moses, 'for John had said unto Herod, "It is not lawful for thee to have thy brother's wife"' (Mk 6:18).

The Lord's answer to the two disciples was, 'Go and tell John'. Wonderful things were happening. The explanation could only be that there was a visitation from heaven. To account for the blind receiving their sight, and the lame walking; lepers being cleansed and the deaf hearing; the dead being raised and the poor having the gospel preached to them, in any way, other than divine intervention was beyond all reason.

The Lord did not say, 'Go and tell John to read Isaiah 35:5', but He gave credence to the prophetic word by describing the signs. John, who was conversant with the scriptures would need no further proof. It was enough for him, and it should be enough for all others who have doubts; the work of the Lord goes on and the evidence of it abounds on every hand.

If a paraphrase may be allowed, it might read, 'Go and tell John, 'keep going on, you know what the scripture says, and it is all happening'.'

Whether it was due to lack of space, or lack of something to say, or whether Quartus came to Paul's mind as the epistle to the Romans was ending, there is certainly very little said about him by way of commendation. He just goes down on the page of Scripture simply as Quartus, a brother, or perhaps more accurately, Quartus, the brother. His name is the last one in a great list of worthies of the past who are mentioned in what has become a roll of honour, men and women of the first century who took their stand for Christ and who have been given mention in the book which will stand for time and eternity.

If it were possible to have all the worthies of Romans 16 assembled for

presentation, there would be little need to mention now the words which are attached to their names. Countless believers could add the apostle's commendations as soon as their names are mentioned. To Gaius would immediately be appended, 'mine host'. His hospitality to Paul and to the whole church will never be forgotten. At the name of Erastus, the ready response would be, 'chamberlain of the city'. The notice of the fact might seem superfluous to some or even a trifling matter, but it meant much to Paul. Without doubt Erastus was a person of distinction who had taken his stand with the early believers, something which would inevitably draw reproach.

Last of all in the lengthy list comes Quartus. He was one of the brethren. Tradition has marked him out as one of the seventy sent forth by the Lord, but Scripture makes no mention of that. He is to be remembered as 'the brother', and there is a great mine of wealth in that plain fact. The tragedy of modern times is the move away from the stigma of it. Happily, there are many who consider it a great honour to be remembered as a brother, one of a company of brethren who are faithful to the testimony to the Lord in the day of His rejection. Great ones of earth pass on with little mention, but the granite headstone which will stand the test of time is Romans 16, erected to the memory of faithful servants, especially the last one of whom little is recorded, 'Quartus, a brother'.

Fulfil ye my joy, *that ye be likeminded, having the same love, being of one accord, of one mind.* Philippians 2:2

---

*T*he apostle's plea in Philippians 2:2 is not a request for responses that would give him joy; he had joy. It was an appeal to make his joy replete, to fill it up, to leave no empty spaces in his joy before the Lord. If he could have borrowed the words of his Lord he would have strengthened his appeal further, 'good measure, pressed down, and shaken together, and running over' (Lk 6:38).

On either side of Paul's plea there are four certainties. Not doubts, as may be construed from the four-fold mention of the little word 'if' in the first verse, but positive realities. If the verse were loosely paraphrased it would read, 'If there is such a thing as comfort in Christ (and there is), if there is such a thing as love's consolation (and there is), if there is such a thing as a common bond in the Spirit (and there is), if there are tender mercies and compassions (and there are), then I appeal to you all through these verities to fill up my joy to the brim.

The question anticipated by Paul was how to respond to the four-fold appeal. The next verse gives a four-fold answer. The apostle's joy would be crammed full if the Philippians expressed full concord by thinking the same thing, by having the same self-sacrificial love, by being one in heart and soul, by having a mind that was unity itself.

Paul is not on earth now. It would certainly have given him more joy (if that were possible), to think that others down the years would take up his appeal to the Philippians and respond in such a way that strife and vainglory would be buried out of sight. Paul's plea 'fulfil ye my joy' was never more relevant. We would all do well to respond to it.

For **our light affliction**, *which is but for a moment, worketh for us a far more exceeding and eternal weight of glory*... 2 CORINTHIANS 4:17

*T*here are many verses in the Scriptures which are taken up by Christians and without conscious effort are settled in the memory. The reason for this may well be that the grandeur of the thoughts expressed cause an indelible imprint to be made on the mind. For example, few need any help in completing Romans 8:28, 'And we know that all things work together for good...' Second Corinthians 4:17 is one of these verses. It is a well-known and much loved resource for all who find the pressure of daily living difficult to accept and it is therefore worthy of a little consideration.

Paul did not mean to convey to the Corinthians that affliction was but for a moment. He was not thinking of the duration of life's pressures but rather that they were here present and should be considered against eternal glory. Paul's afflictions, which he himself details at great length, could never be dismissed as light or of short duration, but compared with a future weight of glory they were insignificant. In fact, this may well be the secret. The present is light affliction; the future is weight of glory.

The thought on Paul's mind was not to stress merit, as if affliction in life was earning eternal reward. He was resorting to his practice of using superlatives of language, and by drawing on his knowledge of Hebraisms he really soared. Said he, 'The light affliction of the present, more and more exceedingly, excessively to excess, an eternal weight of glory works'. The final result is beyond question. The light affliction of the present time is working out, bringing to the goal, more and more exceedingly, an eternal weight of glory.

There is no need therefore to try and calculate or guess in the present the weight of future glory. The light affliction endured will do its own work, working out, as Paul states, excessively to excess what is sure and certain.

*F*rom what appears to be an ordinary greeting to a man named Rufus and his mother (Rom 16:13), there develops a most intriguing consideration. It is the identity of Rufus that opens up the possibilities of being able to decide who his mother was, and what influence she had on the apostle Paul and the testimony in particular. In Luke's account of the events leading up to the crucifixion of the Lord he records that the cross was laid on a man, Simon a Cyrenian. It is not an account of a man who offered to carry the cross, he was compelled to carry it, as Luke notes, 'on him they laid the cross, that he might bear it after Jesus'. Inestimable privilege it was, although one cannot but wonder what initial impressions were made upon him as he walked behind the Lord.

In Mark's account of the crucifixion scene, he states that the Roman soldiery compelled one, Simon a Cyrenian, to bear the cross, and, what may be taken as a casual reference, remarks, 'the father of Alexander and Rufus'. In fact, the way Mark inserts the reference it seems that the relationship was so well-known, he did not need to expand upon it. Simon had two sons, Alexander and Rufus, and when Mark wrote, their prominence was such amongst early Christians that he merely had to mention their names. The conclusion at this stage is that being compelled to carry the cross had left an indelible impression on Simon and on his sons also.

The question springs to mind, what about Simon's wife, the mother of

Alexander and Rufus? Had she been won over? The possibilities are strong that the answer to the question is found in Romans 16:13, 'Salute Rufus, chosen in the Lord, and his mother and mine'. Of Rufus the Scripture is silent as to what kind of service he carried out for the Lord. Much could be suggested from the statement, 'chosen in the Lord', but there is no conjecture required for determining his mother's role — she was a mother to Paul. It is not that the great apostle was being soft, it was a genuine acknowledgement of his indebtedness to a service which only a woman could supply, and it was tenderly included in a reference to a brother, 'Salute Rufus…and his mother and mine'.

*And whatsoever ye do, **do it heartily**, as to the Lord, and not unto men…*
COLOSSIANS 3:23

There are some very interesting translations of the opening words of Colossians 3:23. The King James Version renders the passage, 'Whatsoever ye do, do (it) heartily'. J.N.D. translates it, 'Whatsoever ye do, labour at it heartily', stressing the need to put some real effort into what is done for the Lord. Rotherham takes the exhortation a stage further and he places the words in his version according to the way he thinks they are emphasised in the Greek text, 'Whatsoever ye may be doing, from the soul be working at it'. Kenneth Wuest in his 'Expanded Translation' considers that the expression should read, 'Whatever you are doing, from your soul do it diligently'.

Each rendering of what at first sight seems to be an ordinary little exhortation, turns the words of Paul round and encourages a closer look at what is being done for the Lord. Whatever is being done, is done more earnestly if labour is expended in the doing of it. Whatever is being done is done more devotedly if it is done from the soul, and if diligence is included it all adds up to acceptable service. And just to ensure that the service is not misguided, Paul points in the right direction, it is 'unto the Lord and not unto men'.

Although the verse could very well stand on its own, it is connected to the next one by a present participle, 'knowing that of the Lord ye shall receive the reward', or better, as the R.V. has it, 'knowing that from the Lord, ye shall receive the recompense'. Labour expended for the Lord is not wasted energy. Devoted service is not a misplaced life spent diligently on a lost cause. Paul states with all authority, 'you will receive back in full, by way of just recompense, a portion of that inheritance which is reserved for you'. And just to make sure that there are no mistaken ideas of whose work he is writing about, Paul adds, 'Ye serve the Lord Christ'. If we borrow an expression from the epistle to the Romans and ask the question, 'What shall we say then to these things?' the answer must surely be, 'Whatsoever ye do, do it heartily as to the Lord'.

*And I entreat thee also, **true yokefellow**, help those women which laboured with me in the gospel, with Clement also, and with other my fellowlabourers, whose names are in the book of life.* PHILIPPIANS 4:3

The identity of the person referred to in Philippians 4:3 as 'true yoke-fellow' is not known. It could not be Lydia since the word in the original is in the masculine. The suggestion that it was a proper name (suzugos) has little in its favour. It is more likely that Paul, who knew the man, was making a play on the words by addressing him 'yoke-fellow, genuine-so-called'. There is no doubt that Paul was registering his praise of this unnamed worker. His appeal is in the word rendered 'help', which has more to it than a passing favour. The ability of the person to help goes without saying. The willingness to help seems also to be understood in the word. The resources behind the true yoke-fellow are taken for granted, so what was Paul concentrating upon? It seems clear that this genuine person had the tact which was necessary and the confidence of the women he was asked to help. Tact is not an asset which is built up overnight. A genuine yoke-fellow takes many years in the making but his worth is beyond measure.

The little company named in this verse has quite a few anonymous people in it. Paul is there of course, and Clement is named, but there is also the true yoke-fellow, and then the women who laboured with Paul in the gospel, and finally the other fellow-labourers at Philippi. Of this last group, and no doubt including all the other named and unnamed servants, Paul adds, 'whose names are written in the book of life'. The law, the psalms and the prophets all have a mention of books in which names are written. It was not a fresh revelation Paul was giving. He was reiterating a well-known fact — God keeps records. Although genuine yoke-fellows, women who serve the Lord and fellow-labourers are not widely known down here, their names are in the book of life and there is no possibility to having them erased. Having therefore that confidence, it is good to look around; yoke-fellows, genuine-so-called, may be in short supply but they are there alright.

' . . their names are in the book of life

and there is no possibility

to having them erased.'

'In times of stress there
are the ones who will
stand, because they have
been through the fire
and have not failed.'

*I*n Paul's second epistle to Timothy he urged his young friend to strive diligently to present himself approved unto God. Paul was not suggesting that there were times when God was unaware that Timothy was a workman in His service. He was placing the onus on him to demonstrate to God that he was tried and approved, someone who had passed every test with flying colours.

Peter has a similar thought. In his second epistle he wrote, 'Strive diligently to make your calling and election sure'. His exhortation turns Paul's in another direction and might be answered by asking a question, 'How do people know that God did not make a mistake when He set His choice upon me and called me by His gospel?' The answer is in the word, 'sure' (bebaios), which calls for the provision of the guarantee by demonstrating christian virtues in every aspect of daily living — against that there is no argument, God's choice was right!

There is no plea attached to the name of Apelles (Rom 16:10). He appears on the page of Scripture, the subject of one of Paul's many greetings. Who he was and what he did is not mentioned. One word tells out, however, where he stood as far as Paul was concerned. It is the word 'approved' (dokimos), a significant word before apostolic times and equally so in each generation since, right down to the present. Metals which have been tried and approved are needed for situations of stress. Their presence is taken for granted, but life would be difficult without them. Paul was not beyond applying the lesson to Timothy. In the spiritual realm, believers who are sound, tried and approved, are needed for carrying out the work. On them the Lord can depend. In times of stress there are the ones who will stand, because they have been through the fire and have not failed. They are, as might be said, sound metal.

In Paul's greeting for Apelles, he acknowledged that he was approved 'in Christ' (Rom 16:10). He was in the same company as Urbane, 'our fellow-helper "in Christ"' (Rom 16:9). Perhaps the expression means relationship. It may carry the thought of being in Christ's inner circle, near and dear to Him. Whatever it means, there was One who knew all about Apelles — he was tried and sure, the man for the job! At the mention of his name in any age, the associated words spring to mind, Apelles, 'approved in Christ'.

*T*here is a sense in which every Christian can be described as a servant of the Lord. Positionally this is correct and it is a very comforting thought to know that there are no redundancies in His service. Once engaged by the best of masters, that happy privilege is secure in this world until the end of life's journey.

However, this was not exactly what Paul had in mind when he instructed Tertius to write to the Romans, 'not slothful in business, fervent in spirit, serving the Lord', or, as it might be rendered, 'in zeal not slothful, in spirit burning, the Lord serving' (Rom 12:11). The service he was drawing attention to was the discharge of the duties of a slave. It was a reminder that work for the Lord was not really optional. The relationship being stressed was one of Master/bondslave, the permanent relation of servitude to another, a case of one whose will is swallowed up in the will of another. In this service there is no question of acting like the man in the parable of Matthew 21 who said, 'I go, Sir', and went on. It is rather a readiness to serve at all times, toiling with a zeal that is worthy of the One in whose royal service all Christians are engaged.

An interesting point about the expression, 'serving the Lord' arises from the field of textual differences. Some manuscripts render the verse, 'serving the time', or, 'serving the hour'. If this reading is adopted, another challenging thought arises. If Christians are bondservants of the hour, the hour of opportunity, there will not be much free time left to fritter away on things which have little or no importance for eternity. Each hour will be identified as having a claim, and since all Christians are bondservants, the demands cannot be shrugged off. Whichever rendering is taken, and both make good sense, the challenge is there to be faced; all are under an obligation to serve the Lord while there is yet time — the hour of opportunity may not last much longer.

*Rejoicing in hope; **patient in tribulation**; continuing instant in prayer...*
ROMANS 12:12

*L*ife's tribulations generally come from two sources, either people or circumstances. The Bible has two words which describe the attitude Christians should adopt when the pressures of life become heavy enough to cause concern. When troubles come from people, 'longsuffering' (makrothumia), is the word which covers the proper response. Instead of being 'short-tempered', which may well be justified, the grace which is called for is long-suffering, a forbearance which is an evidence of the spirit-filled life. It may not be easy, but it is what is expected.

*There is grace,
however,
which gives
ability to bear
the pressures*

The words 'patient in tribulation' are not ones which direct attention to people: it is a plea to give the correct response to adverse circumstances. The short, but pointed exhortation is participial; it is a constant attitude to things, come what may. It does not mean a morbid resignation, as if the pressure is so great that it cannot possibly get worse. That may turn out to be the case, but there is no encouragement in the Scripture to adopt that attitude. The tide of events will flow, but Christians are not expected to sit down in despair and let the waters flood over them.

Paul's short plea is full of meaning. He acknowledges that there are tribulations. There are pressures which come upon the saints. There is grace, however, which gives ability to bear the pressures, and in the bearing of them, turns them into triumphs. The patience called for in Romans 12:12 is a conquering patience. It is the spirit which no circumstance in life can defeat. It describes a fortitude which copes triumphantly with life's events and turns them into glory. It is not a grim struggle, but a radiant approach to life, even in the darkest hour.

It may be that Paul knew that the response he was calling for was what modern language describes as a 'tall order'. That may be the reason why he put a softer exhortation on either side of it, also participial clauses — 'rejoicing in hope, continuing instant in prayer'. There can be little doubt that the apostle knew what he was doing. From his own experience of the trials of christian service, he was giving some secrets of the 'grace of going on', to which may be added the words of Psalm 71:16, 'I will go (on) in the strength of the Lord God'.

*...and the king sent after the host of the Syrians, saying, **Go and see.***
2 KINGS 7:14

He saith unto them, How many loaves have ye? **Go and see.** MARK 6:38

*T*here are two references in the Scriptures to the words of direction, 'Go and see', one in 2 Kings 7:14 and the other in Mark 6:38. Both concern hungry multitudes. In the first, the king of Israel scorned the news that a day of good tidings had arrived and that there was provision for all at the gate of his city. And so it was with great reluctance that he said, 'Go and see'. In the second, the Lord commanded His disciples to 'Go and see', so that they would take into account the meagre resources that were available and from which all would be fed and satisfied.

Despite the rise in ungodliness in the world, it is still a day of good tidings. The gospel is being preached, and like the times described in 2 Kings 7, the blessing is, as it were, at the gate of the city. In New Testament language, Paul makes it plain in his epistle to the Romans, 'The word is nigh thee, even in thy mouth and in thy heart, that is, the word of faith which we preach...' The doubts the king of Israel had about the message the four leprous men preached did not affect the issue. Even although the messengers had no acceptance in society and what they declared seemed too good to be true, it was factual, because they had sampled it themselves. In addition, these outcasts acknowledged that they 'did not well if they held their peace' (2 Kings 7:9).

In the desert place, with the day far spent and little or no prospect of help arriving, there was a feeling of unbelief amongst the disciples. The

The purpose of the Lord in commanding His disciples to 'Go and see' was to prove to them that the answer to the problem was not in men or in things around them, it was in Him.

magnitude of the problem and the meagreness of the resources caused them to express doubts and they did that in no uncertain language. Some miracles they could accept but the situation they were in was, to their way of thinking, beyond the power of the One in whose service they had enlisted. The command, 'Go and see' only confirmed to them at that stage that there was nothing more available than five loaves and two fishes.

The attitude of the king of Israel is typical of many. In his worldly wisdom he thought he saw through it all — it was a trick! His command to 'Go and see' was meant to prove that he was right, but he was wrong. The purpose of the Lord in commanding His disciples to 'Go and see' was to prove to them that the answer to the problem was not in men or in things around them, it was in Him. From meagre supplies a great need was about to be met. As it was then, so it is now, there is still a great need to be met. If how to meet it seems impossible it is wise to 'go and see', and never at any time forget — there is nothing too hard for the Lord!

Therefore, my brethren dearly beloved and longed for, my joy and crown, so **stand fast** *in the Lord, my dearly beloved.* PHILIPPIANS 4:1

*A*mongst many hundreds of exhortations in the New Testament, there is a very interesting one which centres around a word represented by the two words, 'Stand Fast'. When the word is used in the imperative mood, the exhortation does not leave any room for manoeuvring. The tendency in many to argue, reason, or doubt when faced with a direct command has no support when the charge is given to stand fast.

The exhortation to the Galatians to 'stand fast' in the liberty wherewith Christ had made them free was a very demanding one. The Christians, who had received the gospel with joy when Christ and His crucifixion had been placarded before them, were in danger of returning to bondage. For them it was the bondage of law-works, the addition of Judaistic teachings to supplement the work of Christ.

In a wider sphere, the plea to stand fast affects more than the Galatians. Any teaching which endeavours to add or take away from the finished work of Christ must be resisted. Believers have been brought into liberty. It is a freedom which relieves them of any obligation to observe rules and regulations, but it is not a license to do what is not sanctioned by the clear teachings of the New Testament.

Another example of the word in the imperative mood is the one included in Paul's letter to the Philippians. It is introduced by the word, 'Wherefore' and it makes its appeal to believers who are described as 'dearly beloved'. They were to 'Stand fast in the Lord' (4:1). The 'wherefore', or clearer, 'so that', looks back to the dangers outlined in Philippians 3:18,19. There were some, who, in their falling away, had become 'enemies of the cross of Christ'. The only safeguard from the class described so clearly was to stand fast in the Lord. The Philippians were to keep line, present an unbroken front, and do so 'in the Lord'. The maintenance of christian fortitude apart from Him would be impossible.

There is no scope in the exhortation to 'stand fast' for platitudes. Trite sayings which water down plain statements must be rejected. The need for believers who will take a firm stand for what they believe was never greater, so in these evil days, the call comes, 'stand fast'.

. . . *the call comes, 'stand fast'*

*So Daniel was taken up out of the den, and no manner of hurt was found upon him, **because he believed** in his God.* Daniel 6:23

Towards the end of the last century, the prophecy of Daniel came under heavy fire from the critics. The prophet, who had survived the den of lions without a scratch, was once again under attack, but this time from a far more dangerous foe. The Higher Critics wanted to consign him and his doings to the realms of mythology. A doughty campaigner at that time, Sir Robert Anderson, rose to the prophet's defence, and right well he did it in his book, *Daniel in the critics' den*. But, whether in the lions' den or under the critics' pen, the prophet came out unscathed.

'Because he believed' in Daniel 6:23 is a very striking expression, one which has proved to be a blessing to many down the years. Of course, what is recorded in front of the words 'Because he believed' and what comes after are needed to give the statement meaning. As far as the prophet was concerned, when he was taken out of the den there could have been no other outcome than what is stated in the verse, 'no manner of hurt was found upon him, because he believed in his God'.

Exactly what Daniel believed is not stated. There is no evidence that he knew that the mouths of the lions were shut by divine intervention, and it is doubtful if he had a precedent of a similar nature to guide him. What is clear, however, is that he had a sterling faith in God, which rolled the matter on to Him. Even if the lions had been capable and inclined to attack, Daniel's faith would not have wavered; it was God's business.

The circumstances which provide the reason for the statement of Daniel's faith may not be the experience of many today. Lions in their dens, or out in the open for that matter, are not generally what Christians have to face to prove the reality of their faith in God. But trials abound, nevertheless, and serious ones at that which call for total reliance on the living God. Many of God's servants find themselves in the critics' den as they seek to serve. Some find that they have Daniel's problems but are not so sure about having Daniel's assurance. And, it is evident, doughty campaigners are not always at hand to defend. Nevertheless, a firm stand for God must produce results. As with Daniel, be it the king, or any others who oppose, they will find that believers have an uncanny ability to turn adversity into victory. And why should it not be? God has not changed! Daniel triumphed **because he believed in his God.**

*I therefore so run, not as uncertainly; **so fight I**, not as one that beateth the air...* 1 CORINTHIANS 9:26

here are some who consider that Paul's imagery in 1 Corinthians 9:26 is hardly in keeping with the message of grace which he made known. Running in a race with the express purpose of winning the prize has all-round acceptance as a metaphor, but engaging in pugilism seems out of place and perhaps even contradictory as far as the principles which govern christian living are concerned. Of course, in the Grecian games, to which the apostle refers, racing and pugilism featured prominently, and both called for the utmost effort on the part of the participants.

Everything Paul did was for the gospel's sake (9:23). If it were right to apply a motto to his way of life it might be suitably rendered in the words of verse 22, 'that I might try by all means to save some'. In pursuance of that goal, however, indolence and self-indulgence were entirely out. Self-denial and self-discipline were demanded and to this end a warning was addressed to the Corinthians. They were bringing their own state before God into question; hazarding their souls' welfare by their worldly practices.

Paul's vivid thinking takes him into the race. He is temperate in all things, keeping his body in subjection. In this confidence he then writes, 'I therefore *so* run, not as uncertainly'. He will run strictly in accordance with the rules (2 Tim 2:5), and he will do so with the prize in view. From the metaphor of running he turns to another, '*so* fight I' He considers himself as the pugilist, making every blow tell. The tactician in him deplores the thought of flailing fists that beat the air and accomplish nothing. In the spread of the gospel every word for every soul must count. One way or another, a savour of life or a savour of death, every blow must register.

The apostle's concern does not end with entering the race or engaging in the fight. 'I therefore *so* run', and '*so* fight I' have a solemn ending. After all his effort, he fears that he might be disapproved. The possibility of being amongst those who ran but did not obtain the prize was ever with him. Nevertheless he ran, and he fought, and he left the awards to the Umpire.

If any of you lack wisdom,
let him ask of God, that giveth
to all men liberally, and
upbraideth not; and it shall be
given him. JAMES 1:5

*I*t come as a surprise to many that there is a wisdom from beneath and a wisdom from above. Both of these are recognisable by certain characteristics and they are listed by James in his epistle. Concerning the wisdom from beneath there are two features in particular which are striking. Firstly, it is said to be earthly, that is, it has no horizons beyond the boundaries of earth and it has no appreciation of values which are spiritual. Secondly, it is described as being soulish, it is marked by animal cunning.

Happily there is another wisdom. It is that practical prudence which Solomon asked for and which is still on offer to Christians according to James 1:5. Here the promise is that a petitioner can keep on asking and a giving God will bestow liberally. He will do it in abundant measure without reserve, or as an old version of the Scriptures has it, 'He will not cast it up in your teeth'. Perhaps James was one of those who sat and listened to the sermon on the mount and heard his Master say, 'Ask, and it shall be given you', or as it might be rendered, 'Keep on asking and it shall be given you'. God will not be wearied by His saints who keep on asking, nothing doubting of course.

Some say that James lists ten marks of the wisdom from above. This may be so and it is good to know that they are the ingredients of the heavenly wisdom which God is anxious to impart to His saints. Amongst these many graces there is one which is worthy of special note. It is rendered in the Authorised Version as 'gentle' and may be further described as suitable, mild, or fair. It is interesting to note that the word is said to be the most untranslatable word in the New Testament. One has suggested that it goes beyond a person who stands up for his legal rights, and adds this comment, 'If God stood on His rights what would become of man'? How interesting to know that in the wisdom from above there is a feature that is sweetly reasonable, even to the point of being satisfied with less than its due. It is just another indication that the wisdom from above includes a striving after the best ends and uses the best means to obtain them. There is nothing difficult about it — just keep on asking God!

*As every man hath received the gift, even so minister the same one to another, as good stewards of **the manifold grace of God**.* 1 Peter 4:10

The New Testament has a word of fairly frequent occurrence, which in itself is of no great significance. When, however, it is attached to certain other words it assumes special characteristics. The word is *poikilos*, which is rendered on several occasions as 'manifold', meaning *all-varied*, like Joseph's coat; it was a coat of *many* colours.

The apostle Peter has two references to *poikilos*. He writes firstly of manifold temptations (1 Pet 1:6), and then of manifold grace (1 Pet 4:10). In the first he recognises that some are in distress because of life's many testings. He does not deny that in the christian life trials of every shade and shape come fast and furious, and these can cause inward and outward grieving. The fact that they are there for the proving of the believer's faith does not always bring home to the sufferer the promised consolation, although it must be stressed that it is never far away.

If the trials of life are all-varied, and there are few who will deny that the variety seems endless, it must also be recognised that there is not a trial for which God has no answer in grace. Paul had another way of expressing this provision and he passed it on to the Corinthians. Said he, in effect, 'You may find yourself in what looks like a cul-de-sac with no way of escape, but let me tell you that there are no blind alleys in the service of God. Every dead-end has an egress, a way of escape, a trap door: if that were not the case, God would be found to have limitations and that could not bear thinking about.'

Although the meaning of *manifold grace* in 1 Peter 4:10 associates all-varied grace with the exercise of spiritual gift, the fact remains that every form of trial and temptation which can confront a Christian, has an answer in the manifold grace of God. It does not matter how varied the problems of life may be, the grace of God is ever and always more so. It must surely be, therefore, that comfort and encouragement will be derived from the knowledge that even the valley of despair will not find God searching around for some way to help. His **manifold grace** is an inexhaustible storehouse. It has all shades of colour and cure, and assuredly, one at least for every trial.

*Thou wilt shew me the path of life: in thy presence is fulness of joy; at thy right hand there are **pleasures for evermore**.* PSALM 16:11

There are not many in the world who would not welcome an offer of pleasures, guaranteed to last for evermore, particularly if the pleasures were to commence here and now. Of course, what people of every race consider as pleasurable differs so widely, to satisfy everyone's tastes down here would be well-nigh impossible. There is no difficulty, however, in what the psalmist proposes in Psalm 16:11, for the pleasures he writes about are at the right hand of God. All who are privileged by grace to attain to that will be entirely and eternally satisfied with what they find there.

The psalm which ends in such a high note is a Messianic one, and it has therefore the Messiah as its subject. It is He who is at the right hand of God and finds His pleasure in the position He occupies. The psalm is also a 'golden psalm', the first of six which bear the title, the other five being Psalm 56 – 60. These golden psalms are said to be writings of deep and mysterious meanings, and if that is so, the pleasures at the right hand of God come into that category. It is significant that a description of the form the pleasures will take is not developed; that is a secret God has kept to Himself, but what is certain is that those who will one day discover them will not be disappointed. Indeed, an indication of what is on ahead is given by the psalmist in verse 11, where he states that in the presence of God there is fulness of joy.

While serving the Lord Christ, many of His saints get deeply involved with the things which surround them and make up their sphere of work. Being so busily and legitimately occupied, they find that the pleasures of the future tend to become hazy considerations. In the writings of the psalmist the future is not dismissed with a few desultory comments. An example of his joyful anticipation is given in Psalm 17:15, 'As for me, I will behold Thy face in righteousness: I shall be satisfied, when I awake with Thy likeness.' Regardless of what others thought the psalmist's conviction was clear: there were pleasures at the right hand of God and there was no possibility of the joy of them fading. The eternal freshness of the One at God's right hand will ensure that the pleasures will have no ending; they are, as the psalmist states, 'for evermore'.

. . . he announced with all confidence,

'I believe God.'

*Wherefore, sirs, be of good cheer: for **I believe God**, that it shall be even as it was told me.* ACTS 27:25

There is a great difference between the declaration, 'I believe God' and one which states, 'I believe *in* God'. In the account of Paul's shipwreck in Acts 27 the apostle did not convey to the ship's company what would amount to a profession of faith, 'I believe *in* God'; he made known that he had a specific word from God about the situation and he believed it implicitly.

From the details given by Luke, the message Paul received that not one of the 276 men on board the ship would be lost, was contrary in every respect to what looked like happening. The ferocity of the storm, the breaking up of the ship, the helplessness of the sailors, all pointed to an imminent catastrophe, but the Lord's servant boldly declared, 'I believe God'. What others thought was of little consequence. Some might have had their own gods, but one thing is certain, there was only one message, and it came to Paul with such clarity that he announced with all confidence, 'I believe God'.

Various experts in nautical matters have examined Luke's account of the storm and have confirmed that what he wrote stands up to the closest scrutiny. Luke did not overstate the case. All the details he supplied add up to an exact account of a tremendous storm at sea and in the midst of it all the central figure, as it were, was the Lord's servant. The panic that gripped the sailors did not move him. He had a word from God, and come what may, that was enough for him.

There are few of the Lord's servants in any age who have not found themselves in some kind of storm at some times in their lives. They may not describe their experiences in such graphic terms as 2 Corinthians 11:26,27, 'In journeyings often, in perils of water..., in perils of the city..., in perils of the wilderness..., in weariness, in painfulness, in watchings often', but they have them just the same. How do they cope? Much the same way as Paul, no doubt. They have a word from the Lord in their hearts, 'And lo, I am with you alway' and so they too can say with the apostle, despite the trials of the way, 'I believe God'. There are no idle words in heaven's vocabulary.

The wonderful promise of 2 Peter 1:10, 'Ye shall never fall' is conditional. It is very firmly tied to the preceding statement, 'If ye do these things'. This may be a disappointment to some who would be happy to have the promise on its own, so that, come what may, they will never stumble. That is not the way of things, however. It would be an odd kind of existence if life could be lived with carefree abandon in full assurance of never coming to grief.

Peter was never authorised, or commissioned, to offer total freedom from stumbling regardless of how life was lived out. He had the secret of freedom from falling, of course, but to have it depended upon a certain course of action. The things that he referred to in verse 10 are the virtues set out in verses 5–7. He states confidently, 'if these things be in you and abound, they make you that ye shall never be barren nor unfruitful in the knowledge of our Lord Jesus Christ'. If it is argued that there is a lack of the necessary wherewithal to put the virtues into practice, Peter meets that by declaring that genuine believers are made partakers of the divine nature, with the result that in a Christian's faith there is every grace potentially. All that is required is time and diligence to allow or cause the virtues to develop.

There is a warning, however. Every advance in the christian life widens spiritual understanding. If the choice is made to remain in an undeveloped state, such a person is blind and has forgotten that there was a time when the decision was made to leave the old ways and sins behind. The apostle's advice therefore is to strive diligently to demonstrate that God's electing grace was correct. The growth and shining out of christian graces are the proofs that God's choice was not a mistake. The wonderful outcome must then be, 'Ye shall never fall'.

'If these things be in you and abound,

they make you that ye shall never be barren

nor unfruitful in the knowledge

of our Lord Jesus Christ.'

Now *therefore **give me this mountain**, whereof the* Lord *spake in that day...*
JOSHUA 14:12

*A*t first sight the request 'Give me this mountain' appears to be a strange one. It seems to fit into the same category as the well-known expression, 'Reaching for the moon'. Why anyone would make a request for a mountain is a baffling consideration. And then, what would one do with a mountain even if it were handed over? The appeal was made by a man who was eighty-five years old. By normal standards he was well past the age of retirement and should have been content to meet with his old friends to talk over the great events of former times. The man in question, however, was not past his peak. In his own words he could claim, 'As yet I am as strong this day as I was in the day that Moses sent me; as my strength was then, even so is my strength now' (Josh 14:11). The man, of course, was Caleb and the reason for his request to Joshua was that the mountain was held by the enemies of Israel and that was an affront to him and to the God whom he served.

Caleb's name means 'wholehearted'. Five times in the record of his life it is stated that he 'wholly followed the Lord', and on one other occasion the Lord Himself said, 'he hath another spirit with him and hath followed me fully'. The five occasions where it is recorded that Caleb wholly followed the Lord are worthy of consideration. Each one was at a time of crisis. The Lord Himself was the first to give the commendation (Num 14:24). The second was Moses (Num 32:12). The third was Moses again (Deut 1:36). The fourth was Caleb himself (Josh 14:9). The last was his friend Joshua (Josh 14:14).

With a background like that it is not so strange after all that an aged servant should make a request, 'Give me this mountain'. It was there to be conquered. It might have seemed to be an insurmountable obstacle but Caleb knew it could be taken for God and to go round it was out of the question. Life is like that. Mountains are too high for some. Advancing years are pleaded by others. All that and much more may be true and valid, but the fact remains, there was a man, a wholehearted man, and no obstacle was too big for him. He was God's man for the task — impossible though it seemed!

*And Ananias **went his way**, and entered into the house; and putting his hands on him said, Brother Saul, the Lord, even Jesus, that appeared unto thee in the way as thou camest, hath sent me, that thou mightest receive thy sight, and be filled with the Holy Ghost.* ACTS 9:17

Some of the missions the Lord's servants are sent on are rather formidable at first sight. Indeed, from a human standpoint they may even be questionable, but then, God makes no mistakes and He never sends His messengers on what is described in Scots parlance as a 'Gowk's errand'. When Ananias was commissioned by the Lord to go to a house in Straight Street, Damascus, and lay his hands on a man there, he had an objection. He had heard of the man he was being sent to see, and what he had heard was not pleasant. The man's evil deeds were well known. In Jerusalem many of the Lord's saints had suffered at his hands. To Ananias, a devout man and blameless before the law, such a mission was questionable. The man in the house of Judas in Straight Street in Damascus was blind and to all intents he had received the due reward of his deeds. Why indeed should mercy and compassion be shown to him?

It was not incumbent on the Lord to give an explanation to Ananias. Such is His grace, however, He explained that the man he was to go and see was a special vessel. Great things were planned for him. Great suffering too would be his lot. From that point, the explanation having been given, the plain words of Scripture confirm why this devout man was selected for a task which few, if any, could have handled. The historian Luke records 'And Ananias *went his way*, and entered into the house'. What transpired is not left merely to the historical account. The man who was blind in the house of Judas never forgot the words, or the face of the man he saw when his sight was restored. In his testimony, he paid his respects to him. He was a worthy servant of God and when he was sent on what appeared to be an unsavoury mission, '*Ananias went his way*' (Acts 9:17).

Not every task the Lord's servants are given is dressed up in an attractive form when allocated. Because of this, many are reluctant to accept the Lord's brief. To speculate of the consequences would not be profitable. Far better to be like Ananias of old, who had a question to ask, but nevertheless, '*went his way*'. If he lived to see and hear of the great deeds the special vessel carried out for the Lord, he would no doubt be happy that he went, and just did as he was directed.

My brethren, count it all joy when ye fall into divers temptations...
JAMES 1:2

*J*ames commences his epistle with 'Count it all joy'. Rotherham, keeping close to the order in the original, renders the words, 'All joy account it my brethren', and then the reason is given for the rejoicing. It is when the believer falls into all kinds of temptations and trials.

It is very strange that 'all joy' should be recommended as the correct response to the onset of trials. There are few who would object to 'unmixed joy' as the blessing of God when all things are bright, but to have 'nothing but joy' as the accompaniment of heavy troubles is another consideration altogether. Nevertheless, there is no avoiding the challenging statement which James places at the head of his epistle. He was no doubt writing from experience when he advised those to whom he wrote to make up their minds to regard all types of adversity as something to welcome and be glad about.

It seems clear that James was saying, 'You may not be in trouble now, but make up your minds that trouble will come'. It would be a very naive person who would set out on life's journey with the persuasion that there were no trials and temptations ahead. The proper christian attitude to it all, however, is that the trials will bring rich treasures into life's experiences if they are entered into with God. It is not merely a question of survival, it is one of surmounting. The young bird is not put out of the nest by its parents that it might crash to the ground, but to prove its wings.

So it is with the Christian. Trials will come, that is inevitable. What then is the proper response? The counsel of James is clear. It is to count it all joy when they do come because God has ordained that they are for the proving of faith. And when the process is accepted, the servant of God will be moving towards the ultimate, which is, as James notes, 'Perfect and complete, lacking in nothing'.

*Whereas ye know not what shall be on the morrow. For **what is your life?** It is even a vapour, that appeareth for a little time, and then vanisheth away.* JAMES 4:14

*T*he question, 'What is your life?' posed by James in his epistle (4:14), has been asked on countless occasions since apostolic times. Preachers and teachers have concentrated on it to impress upon their hearers the brevity of time. In this, of course, they have been quite correct. Life at best is very brief, as the well-known hymn so plainly states. In sober moments, therefore, few would take exception to the apostle's reminder that life is like a vapour which appears for a little while and then vanishes away.

Although most versions of the Scriptures render the words of James as a question, it may be that what he wrote was really a statement of fact. If that is the case, the apostle was reminding men and women that they were not facing up to the true nature of their life, it was indeed a vapour. A literal rendering of the original would seem to support that view, 'For a vapour ye are — for a little while appearing, thereafter indeed disappearing'. In addition, there was a refusal to acknowledge that it was not within man's ability to know what would be on the morrow.

But why should James suddenly and seemingly without connection in the context of what he was writing introduce the thought of the brevity of life? The most likely answer is that he wanted to counteract the thoughtlessness that was apparant in people which failed to take life's uncertainty into account. He recognised that the desire for gain was driving men and women on to plan without God; to think that the goal of trading and profit was the only thing that mattered in life. As James saw it, the folly of planning for the future without considering that not even the next day belonged to mankind was a risky business.

Another approach to life was required. The proper attitude was, 'If the Lord will, we shall live and do this or that'. God's good pleasure should be regarded as the law, whereby all things, human or divine, are ordered. Taking the uncertain future as a guaranteed ground for planning is most unwise. If every individual asked the question, 'What is my life?' and remembered the words of James, 'It is a vapour', reliance on God for what lay ahead would give greater confidence to move forward.

*Therefore seeing we have this ministry, as we have received mercy, **we faint**
not... 2 Corinthians 4:1*

he expression, 'We faint not' occurs twice in 2 Corinthians 4. In
verse 1, Paul writes with all confidence that because God in His
mercy had imparted a wonderful ministry, there was no fear of fainting. He would
not lose heart. There would be no cowardice with him. He would discharge all
the responsibilities God had laid upon him and he would do it with joy.

There is, however, another side to Paul's bold and confident stance.
Although he and others like him were custodians of a ministry designed by God
to meet every need, it was incumbent upon the bearers of the tidings to be
suitable vessels. There were some who walked in craftiness, and handled the
Word of God deceitfully, but the apostle was not like them. He was not amongst
those who would adulterate and falsify the truth. He disowned any connection
with the unscrupulous characters who were prepared to water down the Word for
their own ends. He would handle the Word as it should be handled and remain
transparent before God and man.

At the end of 2 Corinthians 4 the apostle introduces the thought of the
absence of cowardice again. He writes, 'For which cause we faint not, but though
our outward man perish yet the inward man is renewed day by day' (v 16). The
cause which enables him to write so confidently that he and others will not faint,
is the great fact of resurrection. Since Christ had been raised by the power of
God, so will all His saints be raised. No need to fear on that score. Paul rejoiced
that the abundant grace of God would one day rebound to God's glory.

But there was labour. He could not deny that. The outward man was
wearing out day by day. This was inevitable and it affected saved and unsaved
alike. For the unconverted it was a melancholy fact that there was no renewal of
the inward — it was a decay of everything. For the believer, however, the more
the outward man crumbles, the more the inward develops. For this cause
therefore, 'we faint not'.

*And **he from within** shall answer and say, Trouble me not: the door is
now shut, and my children are with me in bed; I cannot rise and give thee.*
Luke 11:7

he strange little parable of Luke 11:5–10 was put to the
disciples by the Lord in the form of a question. They were
asked to put themselves into a particular circumstance and to consider what
action they would take if they were forced to go to a friend at midnight and ask
for bread. It would seem also that they were invited to think of what their
response would be if they were on the other side of the door in the position of
the man who answered 'from within'.

133

The hypothetical construction of the parable does not lessen the importance of its details. A friend arriving at midnight might be a perplexing embarrassment when the larder is empty, but such was the nature of Israelitish rules of hospitality, something had to be done. Turning to a friendly neighbour for help would therefore seem to be the only logical answer to the problem.

The man petitioned, however, responded roughly. The telling expression, 'he from within' supposes an answer from behind locked doors. Although he was bedded down with his family and was reluctant to rise, he was also governed by an obligation to show hospitality. Nevertheless, as the language of the parable states, 'he will not rise and give him because he is a friend, yet because of his importunity (his shamelessness, his gross impudence), he will rise and give him as many (loaves) as he needeth'.

While the disciples were no doubt considering what they would have done in the circumstances, the Lord made His application. It was a three-fold promise. Unwearied and persevering petitioning will not find reluctance behind locked doors to grant requests. At a far higher level, 'He from within' will not say, 'trouble me not', but will ensure that the asker receives, the seeker finds and the one who knocks on the door will have it opened.

But **the God of all grace**, who hath called us unto his eternal glory by Christ Jesus, after that ye have suffered a while, make you perfect, stablish, strengthen, settle you. 1 PETER 5:10

---

*T*he choice expression 'the God of all grace' is undoubtedly the introduction of a small prayer. In Peter's experience, he had proved to himself that every grace was resident in the God he served. Suffering, as far as the apostle was concerned, was incidental; it was part of the Christian's lot, and, as he notes, there should be joy when reproach comes, for the compensations completely outweigh the trials. And anyway, as is clearly stated, God had not called His saints to suffering — which in any case is only for a little while — He had called them to His eternal glory.

Having established that, Peter then makes known the substance of his prayer. It was four-fold, perhaps even four-square, if its terms are taken as four sides of an imaginary structure. Certainly the four words chosen have all the marks of something fundamentally solid and secure, and they are assuredly not beyond the capabilities of God to grant to His people that they might be steadfast in the faith.

The expression, 'Make you perfect' represents a word of frequent use in the New Testament. Taking all the shades of meaning into account, what is at the core is that God wants to adjust His saints, and He will not carry out a patchwork repair, but will restore as new when occasion demands. Peter knew this. He had

'. . . be glory and dominion for ever and ever, Amen.'

been adjusted many times in his life and he was confident that the God of all grace would do the same for others.

In the same way, he could ask for the establishment of the saints. He was aware that God desired His people to be propped up in the faith and not carried about with every wind that blew. And so he prayed, and he added a plea for strengthening. In this there might just be an echo of the Lord's words. The Saviour had said to Peter on one occasion, 'When thou art converted, strengthen thy brethren'. Such grace could not be ignored, and what surer way to put it into effect than to call upon God to work it out. And then the fourth side of the prayer is added. It was, 'settle you'. He had heard his Lord speak of the house that was founded upon the rock and so he used the same word. It rounded off a short prayer, one of great substance, and so obviously in keeping with the mind of the God of all grace, to whom, as he states, 'be glory and dominion for ever and ever, Amen'.

*And it came to pass, when he was in a certain city, behold a man full of leprosy: who seeing Jesus fell on his face, and besought him, saying, Lord, **if thou wilt**, thou canst make me clean.* LUKE 5:12

The cleansing of the man who was full of leprosy (as Luke notes) has been the subject of countless gospel addresses down the years. In the will of the Lord, the incident will no doubt continue to be taken up by preachers as they try to impress upon mankind the loathsomeness of sin and the power of Christ to deal with it.

There are other lessons to be learned, however, and not the least amongst them being Mark's notice of the compassion of Christ. It is fairly well-known that the thinking of the ancient Greek philosophers on the concept of God was that a divine person could not be manipulated. The reasoning was that if a man could in any way influence God and cause Him to act, then that man had power over God, and God could not therefore be divine. Of course, God cannot be manipulated but the reasoning of the philosophers was seriously flawed. It did not take into account that God could respond quite apart from any thought of manipulation. States the writer to the Hebrews, 'we have not an high priest which cannot be touched with the feelings of our infirmities' (Heb 4:15). It is not manipulation that causes Him to be touched, it is divine compassion that responds constantly to the needs of His saints.

The leper cried out, 'If Thou wilt'. He was not doubting the ability of Christ to cleanse him from his leprosy. He was not trying to embarrass the Lord by testing His willingness in front of a multitude. His appeal was to the tender-heartedness of Christ that somewhere, deep down, there might be a crumb of comfort for him, hence his plea, which could be rendered, 'I beg of you, please, can you do anything for me?'

The note by Mark, 'And Jesus, moved with compassion' is a choice one. The word used denotes a reponse that came from the depths of His being. The word is not associated with others in the Gospels, except as used by the Lord on a few occasions in His parabolic ministry. The leper, of course, did not know what moved the Lord. He simply made his plea, 'If Thou wilt', and stood in all his helplessness, a living proof of the ravages of sin. He did not have long to wait until he found out what countless others have found, and are still finding, that 'the mercy of the Lord is from everlasting to everlasting upon them that fear Him' (Ps 103:17). There is no reluctance with the Lord to bless those who come to Him believing.

> *It is not manipulation*
>
> *that causes Him to be touched,*
>
> *it is divine compassion*
>
> *that responds constantly*
>
> *to the needs of His saints.*

*Let love be without dissimulation. Abhor that which is evil; cleave to **that which is good**. *ROMANS 12:9

*P*aul's exhortation to the Romans to 'cleave to that which is good' and his plea to the Thessalonians to 'ever follow that which is good' must take into account that those to whom he wrote knew exactly what was involved. The words of the apostle would carry little meaning if some mystery surrounded what he wrote. In both cases, however, there does not seem to have been any need on the apostle's part to stop in the middle of his exhortations to explain what he was getting at. He just swept on and made his burden known that he wanted both companies to be fully occupied with what was beneficial to themselves and to mankind in general.

Of course, there are so many things that are beneficial. In the Scriptures it is the context which decides what would be on a writer's mind if he desired to direct attention to something specific. As far as the Romans were concerned, out of about twenty occurrences of the word, rendered 'good', perhaps the statement of 10:15 sums up what is best for mankind in a collective sense. There the apostle quotes from Isaiah 52, 'How beautiful are the feet of them that preach the gospel of peace and bring glad tidings of good things'. What could be better than the 'good things' of the gospel of God? What does God have for this age which takes precedence over that? The more the gospel is understood and appreciated the greater will be the wonder about the far-reaching good it contains.

It is worthy of consideration, however, that different qualifying words were used by Paul when he raised the subject of 'that which is good'. To the Romans he counselled, 'cleave to it' and to the Thessalonians, 'ever follow it'. In the apostle's time the word which he used, rendered in the Authorised Version as 'cleave' was derived from the word for glue. It does not take much reasoning to appreciate what was on the apostle's mind when he wrote to the Romans. Similarly, the exhortation to the Thessalonians to 'ever follow that which is good' is quite clear. The word he used on that occasion contains the thought of pursuing earnestly, ever pressing towards the goal of apprehending that which is good.

It would be very remiss of believers today to gloss over these two short appeals. What is beneficial according to the Scriptures, must occupy both talents and time. All ought therefore to cleave to what which is good and earnestly pursue it.

'How beautiful are the feet of them that preach
the gospel of peace and bring glad tidings
of good things.'

> **Be ye therefore** *perfect, even as your Father which is in heaven is perfect.*
> MATTHEW 5:48

*O*ne of the best-known expressions in the word of God is the command of Matthew 28:19, 'Go ye therefore'. Unfortunately the great commission has been given more prominence in a missionary context than in the wider sphere of service for which it was obviously intended. The disciples who heard it were only the forerunners, they were simply the pioneers who set the pattern for the many who would follow 'unto the end of the age'.

There is another telling phrase in the New Testament, of equal importance, and yet it does not seem to have been given its proper weight. In the sermon on the mount, our Lord set out many principles. They were wonderful statements which had never before fallen on the ear of mortal man. Amongst them there was one which establishes the highest possible standard for all who seek to be disciples of Christ. Said He, 'Be ye therefore perfect, even as your Father which is in heaven is perfect' (Mt 5:48). By using the word 'therefore' the Lord linked the statement to all that He had set before His audience. There was no avoiding the conclusion. The consequence of His ministry had to be faced, and that was, 'Be ye therefore perfect'. Man's frailty could not be used as an excuse for lowering it. Even if the goal stretched out into infinity, it made no difference; there was a standard and it could not be lowered to accommodate any.

In the epistle to the Ephesians Paul used the same phrase. Wrote he, 'Be ye therefore followers of God, as dear children' (Eph 5:1). In this case the deduction to be made, the conclusion to be faced can hardly be confined to the immediate context of being tenderhearted and forgiving. That such a conclusion is true, of course, cannot be denied. Sound exposition would demand it. More likely, however, in a proper handling of the passage, the conclusion to be faced would be a going back to the beginning of the section, commencing at the first verse of chapter 4. At that point the word 'therefore' comes up again taking the reader back to the beginning of the epistle. The lesson seems to be, if any will be followers of God as dear children they will do their best by adhering to all that has been written in the word of God. In that way, the command, 'Be ye therefore perfect' has a better chance of being obeyed.

But Peter said, **Not so, Lord**; *for I have never eaten any thing that is common or unclean.* ACTS 10:14

---

*T*here is a world of difference between Peter's statement, 'Not so, Lord' and the question Saul of Tarsus raised on the road to Damascus, 'what will you have me to do, Lord?' In Peter's case what he was required to do clashed with his religious upbringing and the restrictions of that, he judged, had to take precedence over anything else, even the command of the Lord. As far as Saul was concerned, his religious bigotry received such a shock, he had no argument; he was overwhelmed by the divine presence and he had no option but to lay himself unreservedly at the Lord's disposal.

It is noteworthy that men and women relate more to Peter than they do to Paul. Perhaps it is because Peter's shortcomings are a reflection of their own. Perhaps also it is because Paul was a man apart. He is seldom seen in the Scriptures as falling from grace. He does not reel from crisis to crisis like his fellow apostle. He was chosen to be a special vessel for a special purpose and his pedigree which he set out in Philippians 3 confirmed that he was head and shoulders above his fellows.

But Peter was different in another way. He was impetuous but likeable, and as far as Acts 10 is concerned, it is to his credit that he had gone up to the roof of Simon's house to pray when the Lord spoke to him. Since his objection, 'Not so, Lord' was made while he was in a trance, an ecstatic state which came upon him, there is a tendency to excuse him. Nevertheless, it was still Peter, and characteristically like him too. On another occasion he had said to his Master, 'Be it far from Thee, Lord', as he tried to turn Him from the purpose of His coming into the world. That earned the favoured disciple a rebuke of the sternest kind, 'Get thee behind Me, Satan'.

If the expression, 'Not so, Lord', is considered thoughtfully, it will be seen to be a contradiction of terms. Any attempt to correct Deity or change the stated purpose of a divine Person cannot possibly stand. If the way is clear, but there is an objection to going forward, the two words, 'Not so' are understandable, although inexcusable, but to add another and make it, 'Not so, Lord' challenges the Master's divine rights over His servants.

. . . he was overwhelmed by the divine presence and he had no option but to lay himself unreservedly at the Lord's disposal.

*Peter therefore was kept in prison: **but prayer** was made without ceasing of the church unto God for him.* Acts 12:5

In one of his works in which he discussed preachers and preaching, one of the great preachers of the past stated his views on what he considered to be admissible in captions for addresses. One to which he gave his approval was the telling expression, 'But God'. Although it occurs several times, the portion of Scripture which has made its mark down the years concerns the rich fool of Luke 12. His prosperity led him to say to his soul, 'Soul thou hast much goods laid up for many years, take thine ease, drink and be merry, *But God...*'. What followed then made all the difference to that man's plans for the future.

A similar expression is recorded in Acts 12:5, 'Peter was therefore kept in prison: *but prayer* was made without ceasing of the church unto God for him'. The apostle's position looked hopeless. Not only was he imprisoned but he was delivered to four quaternions of soldiers to guard him round the clock. Any hope of rescue was therefore out of the question.

From the reading of the passage it would seem that there was another round-the-clock activity going on at the same time — prayer made on Peter's behalf by the church. No details of the many requests are given. The narrative simply records the resource of the church in the face of a seeming impossibility, '*but prayer* was made without ceasing'.

Although many will hold that there can only be one outcome to a prayer meeting of this nature, the odd fact is that when their prayers were answered, those who prayed did not believe Peter was at the door. They were prepared to believe it was an angel, and if ready to go as far as that, then anyone could be at the door but certainly not the apostle.

How true it is with so many of God's people who are heavily burdened. The hopelessness of so many situations burns into the soul, and even ceaseless prayer does not eradicate the doubts, even when the answer comes. Is it not so that the two words 'but prayer' can open the door to Ephesians 2:4, '*But God*, who is rich in mercy, for His great love wherewith He loved us...'? If the two words 'but prayer' are put into effect, it is good to remember that there are two more which follow — 'but God'. He is sure to answer.

*Rejoicing in hope; **patient in tribulation**; continuing instant in prayer...*

*I*n what appears to be a rather odd statement, Paul wrote to the Romans and declared, 'we glory in tribulations also' (Rom 5:3). It takes a closer look at the context to realise that his words were not as odd as they first appeared. The very circumstances of life which can be so distressing in every sense, he shows can lead on to deeper and greater experiences of the love of God. They are not necessarily sent by God, but doubtless they are allowed by Him. The apostle saw them as pressures, not to be considered as weights that might crush spiritual life, but experiences which would work out patience. They would bring out in the Christian's life

an increase of conquering fortitude; a triumphant upward path to glory.

The pressures Paul had obviously in mind when he wrote to the Romans were not solely the weight of adverse circumstances as they affect the body. Coping with these is bad enough, despite the apostle's ministry about glorying in them. The tribulations he thought about concerned pressures on the soul. These are the ones which make the deepest impressions. They have spiritual overtones in them and they often leave scars which are difficult to heal.

Nevertheless, whether they affect the body or the soul; whether they come singly or fast and furious, the way to cope with them is clear, and that is, 'patient in tribulation' (Rom 12:12). To lie down in despair and let the trials of life flood over the soul is not the response God expects. What He wants from His people is the fortitude which will turn adversity into triumph. It is the spirit which no circumstance in life can ever defeat. It is the ability to deal triumphantly with anything that life can do. This is conquering patience. This is what is behind the exhortation, briefly but plainly stated, 'patient in tribulation'.

Give none offence, *neither to the Jews, nor to the Gentiles, nor to the church of God…* 1 CORINTHIANS 10:32

*P*rior to his Damascus Road experience, the world of the apostle Paul was made up of two classes — Jew and Gentile. After conversion his view would no doubt change, but he would still see mankind divided, this time consisting of saved and unsaved. However, 1 Corinthians 10:32 makes it clear that Paul in fact saw three groupings, Jew, Gentile and a new dimension — the church of God.

In evangelical circles, most people would consider that the world's population is divided into saved and unsaved and let the matter rest there. In that case Paul's exhortation to 'give none offence' would cover all mankind. Taken a stage further, if divisions were ignored altogether and the world was looked upon as the totality of human beings, an attitude of giving no offence to anyone would seem in the end to fulfil Paul's word adequately. However, the apostle's counsel to the Corinthians should not be dismissed lightly — it called for the utmost discernment. Jews had scruples, Gentiles had scruples and the church of God had a new code of conduct, embodied in a new revelation.

Paul's view was that it was incumbent upon every Christian to take the greatest care to avoid giving offence to any of the three classes he listed. Some might judge that consideration for the different views in society to be well-nigh impossible, an intolerable burden upon the Lord's people as they seek to witness for Him in a hostile world. It is obvious that Paul did not think so. He followed up his charge, 'give none offence' with the bold request, 'Be ye followers of me, even as I also am of Christ'. A little of Paul's persuasion would certainly be no bad thing despite the difficulties of the present times.

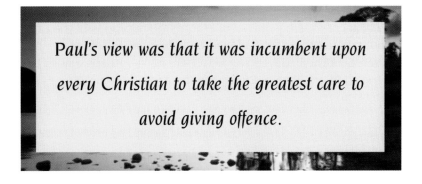

Paul's view was that it was incumbent upon every Christian to take the greatest care to avoid giving offence.

*Hear my prayer, O Lord, and give ear unto my cry; hold not Thy peace at my tears: for **I am a stranger** with Thee, and a sojourner, as all my fathers were.* PSALM 39:12

t was David who wrote, 'I am a stranger', not once but twice   (Ps 39:12, Ps 119:19). They were not the confession of a man who had nothing as far as this earth's goods were concerned; they were the honest assessment of a godly man who had all that the heart could desire, but attached no importance to it. For a king to acknowledge that he was an alien, a foreigner is an indication of the splendour of his own land; the one to which he was travelling. As far as David was concerned, there was no comparison between the present and the future. What lay ahead was the homeland, not the earth in which he admits he was only a stranger.

In Psalm 119:19 there is a plea. Following the acknowledgement that he was a stranger on the earth, David pleads, 'Hide not Thy commandments from me'. Although the things of earth had no hold upon him there was one thing he could not do without. The thought of not having the word of God to guide him caused him to cry out. He was prepared to be a pilgrim provided he had the comfort and consolation of the commandments of the Lord. These were his delight, as he states in his prayer, 'Open Thou mine eyes that I may behold wondrous things out of Thy law'.

The writer to the Hebrews knew about David. He knew also about all the patriarchs before him. They were all in one class, described beautifully in a few words, 'These all died in faith'. Although they lived in a material world they did not conduct themselves according to its standards or its practices, but confessed, 'they were strangers and pilgrims on the earth'. They had faith, a God-given faculty which brought the joys of another world into their everyday lives and enabled them to walk in joyous hope.

Every generation has its peculiar trials. Temptations of the present times may not be dressed in the same garb as the ones of yesteryear, but the issue is the same for the believer. The world will make inroads unless David's attitude to it is adopted, 'I am a stranger in the earth, hide not Thy commandments from me'.

*Preach the word; be **instant in season**, out of season; reprove, rebuke, exhort with all longsuffering and doctrine.* 2 TIMOTHY 4:2

he well-known exhortation from Paul to Timothy (2 Tim 4:2), 'Be instant in season, out of season', has become more of a trite saying with many than the solemn charge it was meant to be. The world has variations of the thought, normally expressed in two words, 'Opportunity knocks'; the general implication being that there should be a readiness to make the most of it when it does.

Paul, however, did not encourage Timothy to sit around and wait for opportunity to knock. His advice went deeper. Indeed, there is one translation which renders the exhortation, 'take or make your opportunity', suggesting that whatever comes, grasp it and turn it to good account, and if no opportunity is forthcoming, go out and make one. This may not always be easy, and perhaps that is why the apostle added the word 'unseasonably', or as the Authorised Version has it, 'out of season'. He recognised that time, as it unrolls its hours and days can be laden with pleasant and fruitful opportunities to serve. He also acknowledged that there are rough patches in between, hence the advice, 'seasonably and unseasonably, be attentive'.

Since the golden rule of interpretation is to take every text in its context, it is essential to follow that principle in 2 Timothy 4:2. Being instant in season, out of season is one of five exhortations, all of which, taken together, place considerable responsibilities on those who would serve God. The previous verse put Timothy under a solemn charge before God and Christ Jesus to carry out the obligations placed upon him and to do it with longsuffering. Patience in respect of persons was essential. Even under provocation christian fortitude was expected to shine through. But, as with Timothy, so with all others, service is not a grim struggle, it is a radiant approach to life. After all, but for the longsuffering of God, there would be no opportunities to be instant in season, out of season.

*P*reach the word; be instant in season,

out of season;

reprove, rebuke, exhort

with all longsuffering

and doctrine.

*And as thy servant was busy here and there, **he was gone**. And the king of Israel said unto him, So shall thy judgment be; thyself hast decided it.*
1 Kings 20:40

To miss out on one of life's vital opportunities can be a traumatic experience. This is made so much worse when it is realised that there is no hope of having another chance. The message of the little parable of 1 Kings 20 illustrates this well, 'And as thy servant was busy here and there, he was gone'. It is the three words 'he was gone' which are fraught with meaning. To be busy here and there may be tendered as a reason, or even as an excuse, but if a vital opportunity has gone and cannot be redeemed, remorse often follows.

Ahab, king of Israel, was given a task. The wickedness of the king of Syria had reached its high-water mark and the sentence on him had been pronounced. God's patience had run out. To the king of Israel therefore fell the responsibility of carrying out the sentence. Gullible, Ahab might have been, vain he certainly was, but it was his spurning of the role that God had given him that caused his downfall. Entering into a covenant with the king of Syria lost for ever the opportunity of clearing up a blight on the land.

To an unnamed prophet was the task given of conveying heaven's displeasure to Ahab. He did it by meeting the king on the road and delivering a small parable, the crux of its message being, 'And as thy servant was busy here and there, he was gone'. It was the king of Syria who had gone and Ahab was responsible. He was not only allowed to go in peace but he went with a covenant in his hand.

Not every opportunity to strike out for God is as serious as the one described in 1 Kings 20, but the principle remains valid. Looking back over lost opportunities the prophet's words can come back with force, 'And as thy servant was busy here and there, he was gone'. How essential it is for all to keep Paul's words to the Ephesians ever before the mind, 'See then that ye walk circumspectly…redeeming the time, because the days are evil'.

Wait on the Lord: *be of good courage, and he shall strengthen thine heart: wait, I say, on the Lord.* Psalm 27:14

*A*mongst the shining examples from the past of those who waited on the Lord, David stands out as the finest. Jacob, Isaiah, Jeremiah, Micah, and even Simeon in the New Testament are noted for special mention in the Scriptures and each one in his day showed calm reliance, waiting patiently for God. David, however, seems different, so different indeed from his predecessor Saul, who could not wait and who has gone down in history for his admission, 'I forced myself therefore, and offered a burnt offering'. His impetuosity cost him the kingdom and despite his pleas there was no scope for repentance.

There are several psalms which give reasons why David waited on the Lord. These are sources of great encouragement for all who find themselves in similar circumstances. How many have been near to fainting through manifold trials, and then had their faith buttressed by the words, 'Wait on the Lord, be of good courage and He shall strengthen thine heart, wait, I say, on the Lord' (Ps 27:14). Of those who have been oppressed, but took to heart the verse, 'Rest in the Lord and wait patiently for Him, fret not thyself because of him who prospereth in his way' (Ps 37:7). Or yet again, those who felt there was no answer to their prayers, until they considered Psalm 40:1, 'I waited patiently for the Lord: and He inclined unto me and heard my cry'.

Although patience is what is most often associated with waiting on the Lord, there are other attitudes of heart and mind also. The psalmist, in addressing his own heart, acknowledged his state of expectancy in Psalm 62:5, 'My soul, wait thou only upon God; for my expectation is from Him'. He had a quiet confidence in God and in His Word, as he notes in Psalm 130:5, 'I wait for the Lord, my soul doth wait, and in His Word do I hope'.

The flesh is impetuous, as most will admit. When it is given room to assert itself, it will lead in the wrong direction. Impatience is not a mark of the spiritual, and when it is felt to be taking over, it is better to wait patiently on the Lord; He will surely answer.

And as ye go, preach, *saying,* The *kingdom of heaven is at hand.*
MATTHEW 10:7

<hr />

*T*he commission given to the twelve disciples in Matthew 10 was peculiar to the time when it was given. They were to go with the gospel of the kingdom and preach it to the house of Israel. It had no message for Gentiles or Samaritans. Any outside the pale of Israel could look to the twelve in vain for help. All the power conferred upon the preachers was for the Jews; it had no wider scope.

Nevertheless, as in all Scripture, there are principles and lessons to be learned and Matthew 10, with its associated passages in Mark and Luke, is no exception. The sending forth, albeit in total reliance upon God for the wherewithal to sustain body and soul, was marked by a simple expression, 'And as ye go, preach'. What they were to preach was explained to them. How they were to behave was made clear. How they were to re-act in the face of opposition was made known in plain statements. In this mission, there was no thought of being sent out at their own charges, everything was covered, and the overriding charge was framed in a simple expression, 'As ye go, preach'.

Going forth to preach in the day of grace might have different conditions but the same Lord is over all His messengers. Like the twelve, the bearers of glad tidings are encouraged to preach as they go, but the scope of the message is wider; it is for all mankind. The same safeguard, however, applies. Whether then or now, the greatest cause for rejoicing is not that demons are subject to the servants of the Lord, but that believers names are recorded in heaven (Lk 10:20). Power is one thing: a registered title in heaven is quite another.

Then answered Peter and said unto him, Behold, we have forsaken all, and followed thee; **what shall we have therefore?** Matthew 19:27

---

*I*t has been remarked often that if Peter had not asked so many questions, much of the Lord's ministry would have been lost to posterity. Seven of these questions are recorded in the Gospels and are worthy of serious consideration. For example, a moment's reflection on the question, 'How often shall I forgive my brother, until seven times?' will automatically bring the Lord's answer to mind, 'I say unto thee… "until seventy times seven".' In the matter of grace, mankind will never outstrip God. Peter's 'seven times' is a reflection of man's best, but how far short it falls of the values of heaven.

So it is in Matthew 19. The rich young ruler seemed genuinely desirous of obtaining eternal life. The stumbling block was his possessions. He could not see them as mere baggage, to be discarded as having no value in settling matters with God. There was apparently no reluctance about 'doing' to sway the balance in his favour, just as long as he was allowed to keep what he had, whether inherited or earned. But it was not to be. The Lord's answer put both 'doing' and 'having' into perspective, 'If thou wilt be perfect, go and sell that thou hast, and give to the poor and thou shalt have treasure in heaven'.

Standing by, and no doubt listening attentively were the twelve. It was Peter, however, who took the opportunity of asking a question on their behalf, 'Behold we have left all and followed Thee, what shall we have therefore' (19:27). In his estimation they had become poor that they might follow the Lord and that must surely earn a reward. Such is human thinking. Sovereign grace can soon be forgotten when a chance to gain something comes along. Nevertheless, God will be no man's debtor and the Lord's reply makes it clear that no sacrifice for Him will be forgotten but will be rewarded lavishly. Peter's question, 'What shall we have therefore?' might have had an element of opportunism in it, but if he had never asked it, the Lord's gracious ministry of encouragement might never have been declared.

*For we would not, brethren, have you ignorant of our trouble which came to us in Asia, that we were **pressed out of measure**, above strength, insomuch that we despaired even of life...* 2 Corinthians 1:8

---

*I*n Paul's writings there are occasions where he uses what some might call extravagant language; words which he seems to have made up to suit the occasion. These words are known as Paul's superlatives. One which occurs quite frequently is found in different contexts and it certainly adds considerable force to what the apostle had in mind to convey to others. In his epistle to the Ephesians he frequently dwells on the thought of grace. In 1:7 he strengthens that by writing about the *riches* of His grace. But even that lovely expression does not convey his thoughts adequately when he contemplates future blessings and so in 2:7 he intensifies the thought further to give one of his superlatives, the *exceeding riches* of His grace.

It is worthy of note that Paul not only used his superlatives to magnify the grace and power of God, he used the same word to describe his own shameful behaviour. In his former life under Judaism, he persecuted the church *beyond measure*, and wasted it, that is, he made havoc of it. If the grace of God was beyond description, this amazing man wanted all to know that what he did in his misguided zeal was in the same category.

Nevertheless, there was no denying the fact that Paul's path as a Christian was a rough one. For many reasons he was forced to describe it in several of his epistles, and not the least amongst these reasons was an earnest desire to encourage others who might find themselves in similar circumstances. His superlative in 2 Corinthians 1:8, *pressed out of measure*, carrying with it a despairing even of life, is always a possibility for God's servants. Many have passed through such a valley and many more, no doubt, will follow. What then is the answer? What would be Paul's word of encouragement? Surely none better than his doxology in 2 Corinthians 1:3, 'Blessed be God, even the Father of our Lord Jesus Christ, the Father of mercies and the God of all comfort; who comforteth us in all our infirmities...in Him we trust that He will deliver us'.

$\mathcal{B}$lessed be God,

even the Father

of our Lord Jesus Christ,

the Father of mercies

and the God of all comfort;

who comforteth us

in all our infirmities...

in Him we trust that He will

deliver us.

For **He knoweth our frame**; He remembereth that we are dust. PSALM 103:14

*T*he short statement from Psalm 103, 'He knoweth our frame', may not raise many eyebrows. At first sight it does not appear to be profound; after all, if God made us, then He must have an intimate knowledge of all the parts, physical and otherwise, which make up the human frame. And apart from that, the fact that God's knowledge is all-embracive may not mean, necessarily, that He will be interested in individuals.

The psalmist, however, did not relegate God to the position of being a disinterested bystander. In this beautiful alphabetical psalm he sets out contrast after contrast between the human and the divine and he does that in a most striking way. Even though he acknowledges that there is always lurking in the background the inescapable fact, 'As for man, his days are as grass', this does not dim the wonderful truth, 'But the mercy of the Lord is from everlasting to everlasting upon them that fear Him'.

But why did the psalmist introduce the statement, 'He knoweth our frame, He remembereth that we are dust'? Was it a morbid acknowledgement of the frailty of man, or the desire to declare his belief in the unshakeable eternal existence of a caring and forgiving God? Taking into account the whole tenor of the psalm, it was undoubtedly the latter. The stress of daily living had its effect on him as it most surely has on believers in this modern age. Tranquility and serenity of life for many is a phantom. The pressures on the mind and body are all too real. But there is comfort and encouragement. The God who knows our frame and who knows all about the pressures that come upon it, has an everlasting mercy which He does not keep to Himself. Perhaps that is why the psalmist begins and ends his psalm with the note of praise, 'Bless the Lord, O

And **such were some of you**: but ye are washed, but ye are sanctified, but ye are justified in the name of the Lord Jesus, and by the Spirit of our God. 1 CORINTHIANS 6:11

*W*hen the apostle wrote these words to the Corinthians, it was not his intention to divide the assembly. He was not identifying a group against whom the others could point a finger and at the same time excuse themselves as not being so bad after all. Neither was he encouraging a morbid recollection of the past, although it certainly enhances the grace of God to contrast former bondage with present freedom.

Although, happily, not all are lifted from the gutter, those who were never there should be swift to acknowledge that if they looked back they would find themselves identified with some class or other in society which was alienated from God. Failure to recognise this is simply a re-enactment of the Pharisee's statement in the parable, 'I thank God I am not as other men are'. It is a very doubtful interpretation of 1 Corinthians 6:11 to limit the washing, the sanctification and the justification to 'such were some of you'. The apostle's statement 'But ye had yourselves washed' must surely refer to the experience which is the common lot of all Christians, regardless of the depth from which they were lifted when the gospel was embraced. In the same way, sanctification and justification are two of the great blessings God can freely give to all who believe as a result of the work of Christ on the cross.

However, the practical application should not be missed. The well-known hymn states, 'What He's done for others, He'll do for you', but from the Christian's standpoint this should be reversed, 'What He's done for you, He can do for others'. The excesses of the unsaved worldwide may cause sorrow of heart, but the remembrance of Paul's words to the Corinthians, 'and such were some of you' should provide the incentive to testify anew to the saving grace of God. After all, there are multitudes in every country whose only hope for eternity lies in their response to the gospel of God.

here are three short forms of speech in the New Testament which are most interesting. The *doxology* is a short, weighty outburst of praise by an inspired penman when he is gripped by the wonders of the revelation he has just written. Some doxologies are very short, such as Romans 1:25, 'The Creator, who is blessed for ever, Amen', and some are of considerable length, such as Jude 24, 25. The *sentence* is a short, weighty, pithy statement which, while related to the text can stand equally apart from the text. A classical example of the sentence is 1 Timothy 1:15, 'This is a faithful saying and worthy of all acceptation that Christ Jesus came into the world to save sinners'.

The third short form is the *benediction*, which is a word of prayer or an expressed desire of the heart to bring down the blessing of God upon one or more whose needs impinge upon the concern of the supplicant. A classical example of the benediction is 2 Corinthians 13:14, 'The grace of the Lord Jesus Christ, and the love of God, and the communion of the Holy Ghost, be with you all, Amen'. It is a great pity that this beautiful form of words is taken up by so many as a mechanical pronouncement, instead of being a guide for the intelligent expression of prayer.

There is also the short benediction of Romans 15:33, 'Now the God of peace be with you all, Amen'. The expression, 'God of peace' is a favourite one of Paul's. To him it was a constant reminder that right relationships between God and man, and between man and man had been established and in the new sphere of peace there was health, welfare, serenity and security. Jeremiah writes of wicked and unjust men who have not known the way of peace, but how different it is with believers of the present age who have come into the blessings of what might be termed 'the Lord's last will and testament' — 'Peace I leave with you, My peace I give unto you, not as the world giveth, give I unto you. Let not your heart be troubled, neither let it be afraid'.

Teach me thy way, O Lord; I will walk in thy truth: **unite my heart** *to fear thy name.* PSALM 86:11

The opening words of Psalm 86:11, 'Teach me Thy way, O Lord' are better known amongst Christians than the closing words of the verse, 'Unite my heart to fear Thy name'. This is the result of the frequent singing of Mansell Ramsey's hymn which begins with the opening words of Psalm 86:11, 'Teach me Thy way, O Lord'.

The psalmist's prayer to unite his heart is a plea to separate it from all the allurements round about him so that his affections would be entirely God-centred. He had no doubt learned from experience, and possibly bitter experience, that the heart was deceitful. If its many fickle desires were followed through, the resulting distractions would certainly break communion with God. On a national scale with Israel this was only too true, the divided heart was a sad reality. But it will not always be so as Jeremiah 32:39 makes clear. The Lord, through His prophet declared, 'And I will give them one heart, and one way, that they may fear Me for ever'.

In the Septuagint, the Greek version of the Old Testament, the plea of the psalmist in Psalm 86:11 is changed and it is rendered, 'Rejoice my heart'. The word used in the Greek text for 'rejoice' is the word which occurs four times in

the story of the Prodigal son to mark the merriment which resulted from his return to the father's house. But why should Hebrew scholars render the text, 'Let my heart rejoice and I will fear Thy name'? One thing is certain, a divided heart will not rejoice in His presence. It is equally certain that a divided heart has lost the fear of His name. Perhaps then the psalmist's prayer, 'Unite my heart' could be accompanied by the plea, 'And make my heart rejoice that I may reverentially fear Thy name'.

The psalmist's prayer to unite his heart is a plea to separate it from all the allurements round about him.

Now therefore go, *and I will be with thy mouth, and teach thee what thou shalt say.* Exodus 4:12

---

here are not many words of direction in the Scriptures which are clearer than those given by God to Moses (Ex 4:12). They followed words of assurance after he had pleaded that he was not really fit to be the channel through whom the Lord would speak to Israel. He claimed to be slow of speech and of a slow tongue, and what he was inferring was that the Lord had made a mistake in choosing him to be His mouthpiece.

There is great grace in the Lord's reply. The divine logic expressed is beyond contradiction and should have been enough for an intelligent man like Moses to confess he was wrong and get on with the work. The Lord's question, 'Who made man's mouth? (and for that matter, the eyes and the ears), have not I the Lord? Now therefore go and I will be thy mouth and teach thee what thou shalt say'. Ths should have been enough. It was in effect a promise that Israel would never be in doubt about the mind of the Lord. Without question, Moses would have been the oracle of God.

But it was not to be. Great man that he was, Moses erred badly. His reply, 'send I pray thee by the hand of whom thou wilt', means in effect, 'send whoever you want, but do not send me'. It is understandable that the Lord's anger was kindled against Moses. The privilege of being the mouthpiece of God was withdrawn and Aaron was brought in. There was no reluctance with him. He could speak well but he was not the Lord's choice; he was at best a substitute. As it turned out, it was not long before Moses rued his decision. If he had obeyed the command, 'Now therefore go' Aaron might not have been in the forefront in the matter of the golden calf. Mankind might be quite happy with substitutes and alternatives, but the second-best is far below God's standards.

'Now therefore go

and I will be thy mouth

and teach thee

what thou shalt say.'

*But Moses' hands were heavy; and they took a stone, and put it under him, and he sat thereon; and Aaron and Hur stayed up his hands, the one on the one side, and the other on the other side; and **his hands were steady** until the going down of the sun.* Exodus 17:12

It was just as well for the children of Israel that the hands of Moses were steady when the battle with Amelek raged. If it had been possible for Joshua and the people of Israel to look up to the top of the hill when they were being forced back they would have seen the hands of Moses had drooped. Good man that he was, he was only human at the best; weariness took over and he was unable to keep his hands up on behalf of the people. When, however, he was given a stone for a seat and Aaron and Hur 'stayed up his hands' the position changed dramatically, 'his hands were steady until the going down of the sun and Joshua discomfited Amelek' (Ex 17:13).

Apart from the many lessons to be learned about Amelek and the reason why Amelek attacked Israel, there is a valid principle which should be taken from the situation. Why was it so important that Moses should hold up his hands? It was because he held the rod of God in it and when his hands became weary it was the rod of God that fell to the ground. That rod was the symbol and pledge of the power and presence of the Lord with the people He had brought up out of Egypt. So it was that after the battle was over and the victory was gained, Moses 'built an altar and called the name of it Jehovah-Nissi' (Jehovah, my banner). The word understood for banner is variously translated, standard, pole, ensign, and was used amongst the Jews for miracle. It was taken by the psalmist and rendered 'lift up' as in Psalm 4:6, 'Lord, lift up the light of thy countenance upon me'.

When the hands of Moses were steady and the rod of God was held up, the light of His countenance shone upon His people. Good it is to remember that victory over the flesh and the forces of darkness is in God's keeping. There is One whose hands never droop and He needs no help from an outside source to keep them up. His steady hands are still in control of every situation no matter how bad things might appear to be.

161

'Sadly, the children of Israel were turned around

to wander in the wilderness. . .'

*There failed not aught of any good thing which the Lord had spoken unto the house of Israel; **all came to pass**.* Joshua 21:45

The four words 'all came to pass' close Joshua 21.

They are remarkable words in a remarkable chapter. In the four closing verses reference is made to 'all the cities', 'all the land', 'all that he sware', 'all their enemies', and finally, 'all came to pass'. All the cities and all the land was what the Lord sware to give to the children of Israel and there stood not a man of all their enemies before them to keep them out from the promised possessions.

Perhaps the joy of Joshua and Caleb was tinged with sadness as they considered that the promised land could have been entered with their contemporaries forty years earlier. The good report that they gave that it was a land flowing with milk and honey was rejected. Despite their word of encouragement, 'Let us go up at once and possess it', unbelief refused to accept it. Sadly, the children of Israel were turned around to wander in the wilderness until all that faithless generation died.

Nevertheless, the failure of the people did not alter the plans of God. He had promised the nation a good land, one which they would hold down for Him. The unbelief in the generation that came up out of Egypt postponed the occupation but it did not alter the outcome. Under Joshua another generation took possession and as the Scripture notes, 'all came to pass' as God had spoken.

Christians, looking back over life, may not be able to identify the many circuitous routes they have taken, but they know they are there. A mixture of unbelief, unfaithfulness and headstrong waywardness has led most, if not all in some measure, to go down the wrong road on many occasions and to refuse to travel on what was known to be the right one. In this there is regret and sometimes remorse, but the saint in touch with God will ever be ready to confess, that despite the faltering 'there failed not aught of any good thing which the Lord had spoken, all came to pass'.

*And he turned to the woman, and said unto Simon, **Seest thou this woman?** I entered into thine house, thou gavest Me no water for My feet: but she hath washed My feet with tears, and wiped them with the hairs of her head.* LUKE 7:44

---

*S*howing courtesy should not be burdensome. To render such grace neither reduces the bank balance nor demeans the status. Some would hold that the display of it is an evidence of good breeding (whatever that may mean). But, as is often the case, those from whom it is most expected are the least ready to dispense it. Such was Simon the Pharisee. Cultured, no doubt. Rich enough too by the standards of his day, but sadly lacking in common courtesy when put to the test.

Simon the Pharisee has gone down in history as the man whose manners let him down badly. As well as earning a rebuke from the Lord, he had to suffer the indignity of having the words, 'seest thou this woman' direct his attention to someone who was making good his shortcomings. No doubt his invitation, his table, his servants, his house, and even his fellow-guests were all of the highest standards, but the things that mattered most were withheld.

Common courtesy should have provided water for the feet. Good manners at least should have provided the kiss of welcome. A readiness to acknowledge a prophet in the midst should have supplied oil for the head. But, sadly, all were repressed. His prejudices stifled his grace and provided an opening for someone with less title to do, and do with more heart, what he had kept back.

In service for the Lord, zeal can sometimes push good manners to the side. A heart for the Lord and a love for souls demand a proper spirit. It does not become the Lord's servants to have the words, 'seest thou this woman' used to give them a lesson on common courtesy. Even in a spiritual way, the teaching of Luke 7 concerning the water, the kiss and the oil should be a reminder that withholding these robbed Simon of the greatest privilege of his life — that of ministering to the Lord.

*After these things the word of the Lord came unto Abram in a vision, saying, **Fear not, Abram**: I am thy shield, and thy exceeding great reward.* Genesis 15:1

*T*he experience of Abram as recorded in Genesis 15 is a season of withdrawal from the path of life. It is what might be termed 'a lay-by' on the road of faith where the cost of what has been undertaken for God is reviewed. Abram needed this. From the moment of his call out of Ur of the Chaldees (Gen 12), until his commendable stance with the king of Sodom (Gen 14), he had been a busy man, but the greatest issue of his life had not been settled; he had no successor.

Before the Lord revealed His mind to His servant, He gave him a word of assurance, 'Fear not, Abram, I am thy shield and thy exceeding great reward'. Doubtless there was a fear in the patriarch that needed to be removed. All that he had as an heir was the steward of his house, and humanly speaking there was no possibility of a child by Sarah. His fear, if that is a correct assumption, was soon dispelled. A look at the stars and a promise from the God of heaven gave him the assurance he required, and so, one of the most far-reaching verses in the Scriptures was recorded, 'And Abram believed in the Lord, and he counted it to him for righteousness'.

The Lord's servants in every age needed to step aside at times and review their position before the Lord. How far have they come, how much have they done and what lies ahead? These matters need to be addressed. To many, all they can see in a Genesis 15 experience which they equate with their own is the horror of great darkness, but the voice of the Lord in the trial is not heard, or the smoking furnace, but the burning lamp in it is not seen. Nevertheless, the Lord is there. Perhaps just a little of the sterling brand of Abram's faith will create occasion for Him to say, 'Fear not, I am thy shield and thy exceeding great reward'.

*And Jesus said, **Who touched me?** When all denied, Peter and they that were with Him said, Master, the multitude throng Thee and press Thee, and sayest Thou, Who touched Me?* Luke 8:45

Three of the evangelist's record the healing of the woman who suffered twelve years at the hands of physicians and was nothing bettered. Taken together, the three accounts make engrossing reading. No doubt the woman was in despair. Hopeless situations bring in that condition. If everything possible has been tried and there is no betterment, despair is understandable.

In the woman's case, reports of a man who had healing powers and compassion to use them had come to her attention. Had he not touched the leper? Had he not touched the eyes of the blind men? Had he not touched the tongue of the dumb man? Had not many sick in the villages and cities touched the border of his garment and were made whole? Then, thought the woman, I can hardly ask him to touch me, but I can touch his garment and I too shall be made whole. What faith! What a testimony to the ability of the Lord Jesus! What a joy to Him to know that simple people with sterling faith were prepared to rely on Him, knowing that all else was hopeless.

When the touch of faith was made, Luke records the Lord's response, 'Who touched me?' The disciples heard and perhaps with a little irritation they say, 'Thou seest the multitudes thronging thee, and sayest thou, "Who touched me?"' That aspect matters little, the one who was intended to hear, heard the words, 'Who touched me' and she came forward. Just one in the multitude. Is it still so that He has time for one amongst so many? His garments are no longer here to be touched, but His touch surely remains. Perhaps the words of William Gaither's hymn expresses it well, 'He touched me, O He touched me, And O the joy that floods my soul! Something happened, and now I know, He touched me and made me whole'.

He touched me,

O He touched me,

And O the joy

that floods my soul!

Something happened,

and now I know,

He touched me

and made me whole.

WILLIAM GAITHER

The three words 'he staggered not' describe the remarkable response of Abraham to the promise of God, 'So shall thy seed be'. Paul's assessment of the patriarch's faith begins with a peculiar statement, 'Who against hope believed in hope'. A literal rendering of the original reads, 'Who beyond hope on hope believed'. Either way, the expression is difficult to understand fully, but it certainly means that faced with the absence of substance for all human hope, he believed with all confidence. It was not a blind irrational response. It was an attitude of mind that acknowledged that the One who had made the promise would bring all to pass according to His word.

So Paul wrote, 'He staggered not at the promise of God through unbelief'. Against the promise of God he did not waver. He knew what he was doing and he did not hesitate for a moment. He was empowered by faith. His absolute confidence in God empowered him to believe the promise and go forward in the good of it. Contrary to what others would have done or what others would have believed, he staggered not at the promise but believed implicitly what God had said.

How God would bring it all to pass was quite beyond Abraham's capabilities to work out, but to his credit he did not even try. He knew his body and that of his wife were as good as dead, but he was fully persuaded that what God had promised He was able also to perform. His faith put him in touch with the One who quickens the dead, the God of the impossible, who can bring forth what He determines out of nothing. Since He is still in control, it behoves His servants in every age to emulate Abraham of whom it is recorded, 'He staggered not at the promise of God through unbelief; but was strong in faith, giving glory to God'.

That in the ages to come He might shew the exceeding riches of His grace
in His kindness *toward us through Christ Jesus.* EPHESIANS 2:7

*I*t is not often that one hears a reference to the kindness of God. This is a real pity as failure to recognise this side of God's nature denies Him the honour that is due from His saints. When attention is drawn to the kindness of God in Scripture, a great word is used. Some times it is rendered 'goodness' and once it is given as 'gentleness' when it appears as the central virtue of nine in the fruit of the Spirit (Gal 5). The Saviour used the adjectival form of the word when He said that the old wine is better (mellow). If that thought is carried over to God's kindness there is an immediate reminder that with Him there is no harshness or roughness, but a sweetness and evenness of temper which sets men and women at ease as he communicates with them.

In Ephesians 2:7 Paul records a wonderful thought. Looking forward to the future, the ages to come, he declares that God is going to make known His kindness to the redeemed through Christ Jesus. By skilful use of superlatives the apostle enhances this thought by stating that God will show the exceeding riches of His grace in His kindness toward us through Christ Jesus. It would have been enough to thrill the heart if the promise had brought out God's grace, but to make it the exceeding riches of His grace in His kindness is really sublime.

Strange as it may seem, this attribute is encompassed in the gospel as it goes out to the unsaved. Men may despise it (Rom 2:4), but using the adjectival form again, Paul states in the same verse that it is the goodness (kindness) of God that leadeth to repentance. People should never presume on God's kindness. As one has remarked, 'Behold His kindness and learn that God is not hard, behold His severity and remember that He is not soft. With God all things are balanced. In His kindness there is no weakness, and in His severity there is no unjustness.'

'In His kindness

there is no weakness,

and in His severity

there is no unjustness.'

But ***they constrained* Him**, *saying, Abide with us: for it is toward evening, and the day is far spent. And He went in to tarry with them.*
LUKE 24:29

*T*here are three words in the New Testament which are rendered in most English versions as 'constrained'. They are not identical words, indeed in many respects could hardly be held to be synonymous. When the Lord constrained the disciples to get into the ship, the constraining there was very different from what Paul wrote to the Corinthians, 'The love of Christ constraineth me'. In the first, the constraining was the compelling of force. The disciples were in danger of being carried away by the plaudits of men and women and their only safeguard was to be removed from temptation. Patronisation is often more dangerous than persecution.

In 2 Corinthians 5:14 the apostle states, 'I am constrained by the love of Christ', 'I am confined, left without an option, hindered from two (sides)', as if to say, 'whichever side you view me from'. He cannot live for himself. The love of Christ holds him in its grip, and he has no choice but to live in the service of others. To that end he had been saved by the grace of God.

The incident involving the two on the road to Emmaus introduces another word and a different thought altogether. It is the same word used by Luke again to make known the compelling of Lydia that the Lord's servants should partake of her hospitality (Acts 16:15). The peculiar force in Luke 24 and Acts 16 is that the compelling will not accept 'No' for an answer. It is the compelling of love expressed in the form of a prayer. It was like the words of Abraham, 'Pass not away, I pray thee, from thy servant' (Gen 18:3). The Lord likes to be entreated by His people. There is little wrong with the earnestness that would detain the Lord and refuse to accept 'No' for an answer. The two on the road to Emmaus did just that.

'Pass not away, I pray thee, from thy servant.'

*And Jesus said, Let her alone; why trouble ye her? she hath wrought **a good work** on me.* MARK 14:6

It is probably too simplistic to draw a fine distinction between two Greek words, *agathos* and *kalos*, by saying that one means good and useful and the other good and beautiful. One has said that a loaf of bread to a hungry person is good and useful, but a bunch of flowers to the sick and downcast is good and beautiful. Few would dismiss that saying as having little merit.

The expression 'a good work' is taken from Mark 14:6. It was part of a rebuke the Lord gave to His disciples (Mt 26), in His defence of the action of a woman in the house of Simon the leper, 'She hath wrought a good work upon me'. The word used to describe what the woman did was *kalos*. It is said that there is no word in the English language which will translate *kalos* adequately, such is the beauty and attractiveness enshrined in it. The anointing of the Saviour by the woman, branded by the disciples as 'waste' was owned by the Lord as a beautiful act. It was timely, thoughtful and sacrificial, just what He needed as the end of life's journey approached. As for the woman, it was a question of 'now or never'. Within a few hours He would be gone and her chance of doing a good work would be gone also.

There will never be a lack of opportunities to do good to the poor (*eu*, to do rightly by them). They will always be there, despite the best of social welfare schemes. Ministering to the Lord, however, is a different matter. Opportunities to do good works to Him and for Him are in the 'now or never' category. It may soothe the conscience in the Gospel meeting to sing 'hasten to meet Him on the way' and yet forget that the hymn has a message for Christians also. If the unconverted need to be reminded that Jesus is passing by, the Lord's people are no less responsible to heed the word. As to the good work, the Lord's commendation of it is worthy of consideration, 'Wheresoever this gospel is preached throughout the world, this also that she hath done shall be spoken of for a memorial of her'.

Who is my neighbour? LUKE 10:29

The question put to the Lord by a Jewish lawyer, 'And who is my neighbour?' is not as easily answered as would appear at first sight. The normal response to such a question, if it were asked today, would take in the person living next door or across the street; the workmate at the next desk or bench; or some other recognised local association. Beyond that, the conception of neighbourliness with its moral and spiritual obligations is not so clear. The question then to be faced is 'How far is one expected to go and what should the response be to those whose behaviour puts them at a distance?' Not all neighbours are neighbourly, all are agreed on that.

Luke's narrative shows that the lawyer knew that the law said 'thou shalt love thy neighbour as thyself' (Lev 19:18). He also knew that as far as the Jews were concerned Gentiles and Samaritans were beyond the pale. Even ordinary Jews were not readily recognised by Pharisees and scribes as neighbours. In order to justify himself, therefore, he raised a loaded question, 'And who then is my neighbour?' The Lord was not expected to have an answer — but He had, and it was a classic.

The story of the good Samaritan has not lost its force. The characters in it were carefully chosen, which makes its application timeless. The Lord's command, 'Go thou and do likewise' implies that neighbourliness does not have restricted horizons. It has difficulties; of that there is no doubt, even insurmountable ones from a human standpoint. Nevertheless, what it is expected from the Lord's servants who claim to represent God in the world, is that they are recognised by others as neighbours, who can be relied upon to respond in a neighbourly fashion when the need to do so arises, even, 'on the road from Jerusalem to Jericho'.

*For my people have committed two evils; they have forsaken me the fountain of living waters, and hewed them out cisterns, **broken cisterns, that can hold no water.** JEREMIAH 2:13*

Some times the Lord's servants are called upon to deliver messages which they know will not be popular. It is of course a test of faithfulness to rise to the occasion and make known the mind of the Lord, even if it means being cut off as a result. Jeremiah soon learned this, but to his credit, he never flinched. Regardless of the status of those to whom he was sent with a message, he delivered what he was given as he received it.

His burden on one occasion was to tell the Jewish nation that they had committed two evils (Jer 2:13). They had forsaken Jehovah, the fountain of living waters and they had hewed out cisterns, broken cisterns, that could hold no water. The inference in the imagery is that God was always near, there was an abundant supply of water in the fountain. That, however, was scorned. God's supply was not required. The preference was for man-made cisterns, which, as Jeremiah was commissioned to make known, held none.

Searching for water when there is none available is understandable, but expending hard labour on a hopeless situation when an abundant supply is readily available is the height of folly. Yet, how many down the ages have done just that. At great cost in time and energy they have dug out cisterns, only to find them in the end broken and empty.

Men and women have to be told, unpleasant though it may be, that the things with which they fill their lives are an offence to God. They are, as Jeremiah states, broken cisterns. God, who has been rejected, is nevertheless standing by, always waiting for a change of heart. The psalmist wrote of Him, 'For with thee is the fountain of life' (Ps 36:9), but there is only one way to appropriate the blessing of that, as the Saviour proclaimed, 'If any man thirst let him come unto me and drink' (Jn 7:37). Hewing out cisterns alongside such a fountain is a futile exercise.

'If any man thirst
let him come unto me and drink.'

Whom having not seen, ye love; in whom, though now ye see him not, yet
*believing, ye rejoice with **joy unspeakable** and full of glory...* 1 PETER 1:8

---

*I*t is common knowledge amongst diligent readers of the English
New Testament that the word 'unspeakable' occurs three times.
Paul writes of an unspeakable gift (2 Cor 9:15) and of unspeakable words (2 Cor
12:4) and Peter tells of unspeakable joy (1 Pet 1:8). What is perhaps not so well
known is that the word rendered 'unspeakable' is different on each occasion. The
unspeakable gift is indescribable; the unspeakable words are unutterable and the
unspeakable joy is inexpressible.

On the grace of giving in 2 Corinthians 8 & 9, Paul considers it from
every possible angle. Despite the complexities of the subject, every aspect can be
grasped by the human mind except the last — that one is indescribable. No one
can plumb the depth of the givingness of God in the giving of His Son.

Regarding the words he heard in Paradise, Paul describes them as
'unutterable'. He is not saying that there was a law which forbade repeating
them, he is making it known that what he heard was restricted to divine usage.
The language of heaven is not the same as that of earth and even to try to utter
the unutterable would be the height of folly. Wrong impressions would result.

Peter's contemplation of the preciousness of faith which is tried by the fire of adversity carries him on to the day of the Lord's appearing in glory. For the Lord and for His servants that will be a day of praise and glory and honour. Peter acknowledges that those to whom he wrote had not seen the Lord, but they believed on Him with an intensity that was inexpressibly joyous. Although there are not enough superlatives in human language to describe it adequately, the joy is real and God must surely take delight in the joy His saints have in His Son. That is not inexpressible as far as He is concerned.

Be of the same mind one toward another. **Mind not high things,** *but condescend to men of low estate. Be not wise in your own conceits.*
ROMANS 12:16

---

*I*n Paul's epistle to the Colossians he set out a very noble occupation when he wrote, 'Set your affection on things above' (3:2). He was really saying, 'Fix your minds on heavenly things', or as Rotherham has it, 'The things on high hold in esteem'. Now this does not contradict Romans 12:16 where the apostle gives the advice, 'Mind not high things'. He was reminding the Colossians where Christ was sitting and where their life was hid, so it was a waste of time and effort to have the mind set on earthly things. Yet strangely he counselled the Romans to condescend to men (or, things) of low estate. Was Paul therefore contradicting himself? If not, wherein lies the answer?

A literal translation of the original of Romans 12:16 could read, 'The same thing toward one another be minding (a call to unity), not the haughty things minding (a call to sober thinking), but to the humble be condescending (a call to true associations)'. Before men and women were on the earth Satan fell as the result of doing what Paul counsels the Romans to avoid. In the haughtiness of his mind Satan said, 'I will ascend above the heights of the clouds; I will be like the most High' (Is 14:14). The result of his high thinking hardly bears thinking about.

Paul's counsel is sound. To be borne alone by humble ways (a true christian grace), or as some maintain, to be one with humble people (both translations are permissible) is not in conflict with Colossians 3:2. It is not an impossible feat to be setting the mind on heavenly things while setting the mind and ways on lowly things. Certain aspects of the christian life may look like enigmas, but happily, things are not always what they appear to be.

'Fix your minds on heavenly things.'

*T*he house at Bethany features in the Gospels of Luke and John. There is no real difference between the two accounts, except for the influence of one person, Martha. Mary's position does not change much. She listens intently to the Lord and then she worships. Lazarus is there but says nothing. It might be expected that being in the resurrected state would have encouraged him to tell of his experience, but his lips were sealed. It was enough that the One who said 'I am the resurrection and the life' was there — anything else would have been superfluous! The difference then between a scene of turmoil and one of tranquillity centres on Martha, but let it never be forgotten, 'Now Jesus loved Martha, and her sister and Lazarus'.

Luke's choice of words to describe Martha's state are like the deft strokes of the artist's brush, a few applications and the atmosphere is fixed. She was cumbered (distraught and over-busied). She was careful (over-anxious). She was troubled (agitated) and in her own words, 'she was left to serve alone'.

Compared with this John's account of the Bethany household had an atmosphere of serenity about it. The different words used by Luke have no place and the only reference to Mary's sister is, 'and Martha served'. It may well be asked, 'What had happened?'

Perhaps the Lord had spoken to her. Perhaps she had a remorse of conscience. In the absence of any information, and conjecture is hazardous, it is more likely that she realised she should be doing what she was best suited for and that is summed up by John, 'and Martha served'. Is this not what Paul advocated in Romans 12:7, 'If ministry (serving) is your gift, get on with the serving'. Happiness will not come by becoming involved in something else, or worse, by interfering with another's work.

If ministry (serving) is your gift,

get on with the serving.

So he sent his brethren away, and they departed: and he said unto them,
See that ye fall not out by the way. GENESIS 45:24

───

*T*his little expression "by the way" is very common in the
Scriptures, but it is only when it features in some significant
happening, that attention is drawn to it. When Joseph said to his brethren, 'See
that ye fall not out by the way' (Gen 45:24), he was not meaning that they should
refrain from squabbling. In patriarchal times they were about to make the most
important journey in the world of that day. The future of the nation of Israel
depended on their arrival. If they had fallen out by the way and failed to deliver
the message to their father, 'Joseph is yet alive and he is governor of all the land
of Egypt', even the coming of the Messiah would have been affected. Happily the
record confirms that they fell not out by the way.

The journey of the two on the road to Emmaus was of the greatest
importance to mankind. No others in the world of that time had the Son of God
as their companion as they travelled. Only two had the experience of 'the burning
heart' as Christ talked with them by the way and while He opened to them the
Scriptures. They started the first sixty furlongs with heavy hearts and no hope,
but the sixty furlongs on the way back were quite different. They were then the
bearers of the glad tidings, 'The Lord is risen indeed'.

Mark records another journey, one of short duration. It was a journey of
shame, and one the disciples would wish to forget. At the end of it they were
questioned by the Lord, 'What was it that ye disputed (debated) by the way?'
There was no answer, 'for by the way they had debated among themselves who
should be the greatest' (Mk 9:33,34). It was not a debate about who should be at
the top of the pyramid (the greatest), but the word has the comparative degree in
the singular. The debate was to settle which one was greater than the rest, no
one wanted to be merely one of the common lot. Such aspirations! One trembles
to think of what each put forward as a title to be greater than the others. But the
disciples are not alone in this kind of debate. How many there are who need
even yet to hear the Lord's question, 'What was it that ye debated by the way?'
Better to have the 'burning heart' experience by the way than be found making a
journey of shame.

Strengthened with all might, *according to his glorious power, unto all patience and longsuffering with joyfulness...* Colossians 1:11

*T*here is a rare expression in the writings of Paul which is 'Strengthened with all might'. Some versions of Colossians 1:11 render it, 'Empowered with all power', since the two words come from the same root. Either way, the sublime nature of the provision is not affected. The might of His glory is available to believers to give divine enabling to do His will. To be equipped with the power is not the exclusive portion of the valiant few, it is there for all God's saints, proportioned to their needs from a supply that is never outstripped by demand.

The verse concerns the glory of Christ. From His place of exaltation He makes power available to His people. In view of this and the promise, 'Strengthened with all might', it might have been expected that this power was for doing great exploits for God. The verse, however, does not limit the power for great feats of heroism, but rather intimates that there is divine enabling for all to live triumphant lives with patience, longsuffering and joy.

There is no denying the fact that the pressures of daily living put a greater strain on believers than the occasional call to do great things. Daily trials and resulting despondency test the powers of endurance. Bitterness, malice and opposition sap the strength and erode the believer's fortitude. But this is not something the Lord does not know about. Extreme pressures call for proportionate power to compensate and this is what is freely available for all that they might be 'strengthened with all might'. After all, the christian life is not a grim struggle. The believer's joy is meant to be joy in every circumstance, not merely in the things that are congenial.

Now I beseech you, brethren, for the Lord Jesus Christ's sake, and for the love of the Spirit, that ye **strive together with me** *in your prayers to God for me…* ROMANS 15:30

*T*t is encouraging to note that apostles were not beyond asking others to pray for them. In Paul's case there are several instances where his requests to various assemblies are recorded. He did not of course commit himself to the Galatians. They were so far adrift from certain aspects of the truth that they needed to sort themselves out before the Lord. There were others, however, recognised by the apostle as having power with God and to them he appealed. To the Colossians his plea for remembrance was that a door of utterance would open up so that he could speak of the mystery of Christ (4:3). To the Thessalonians he appealed for prayer that the word of God might have free course and that he might be delivered from unreasonable and wicked men.

Perhaps the most searching entreaty was the one Paul made to the Romans (15:30). The word he used to emphasise his need of prayer was an unusual one. It is rendered 'to strive together', meaning to fight along with, or to combat in company with any one. It implies serious involvement, engaging in an intense struggle to get through to the Lord. It is clear that Paul was not making request for formal, lukewarm prayer. He anticipated trouble in his service and he wanted the help of fellow-believers. To him, however, anything less than full commitment would not do. The problem he envisaged was too serious for half-hearted endeavour, hence his plea, 'strive together with me'. If the apostle to the Gentiles considered that he needed the prayers of others, how much more everyday believers as they struggle to face up to life's challenges.

And Micaiah said, As the Lord liveth, what the Lord saith unto me, **that will I speak.** 1 KINGS 22:14

*T*he uncompromising stance of Micaiah the prophet (1 Kings 22:14) has a counterpart in Acts 4:20. Micaiah was encouraged to say something that would please the king and his answer was, 'What the Lord saith unto me, that will I speak'. John and Peter were threatened by the council 'that they speak henceforth to no man in this name' (the name of Jesus), and their answer was, 'For we cannot but speak the things that we have seen and heard'.

In Micaiah's case, he was the odd man out. Four hundred prophets were unanimous in their advice to the king. One solitary voice remained to be heard and that was the one Ahab feared. That man's answer was unequivocal, 'What the Lord saith unto me, that will I speak'. John and Peter were branded as ignorant and unlearned men but the proof of the power associated with the forbidden name they bore was there for all to see, the lame man was cured.

The servants of the Lord might be outnumbered, outvoted, and even outwitted; they might be threatened and regarded as ignorant and unlearned, but the fact remains, there is a message to be told out, and told out it must be. The selection of the servant for a specific task is the Lord's prerogative. How he or she is looked upon by others is of little consequence. If God has something to say (and He has) the person chosen to say it has no option. Four words in English settle the matter, 'that will I speak'.

'For we cannot but speak
the things that we have seen and heard.'

*Woe unto you, lawyers! for ye have taken away **the key of knowledge**: ye entered not in yourselves, and them that were entering in ye hindered.* LUKE 11:52

---

*T*he little expression, 'the key of knowledge', occurs in a rather sombre section of Luke 11. Within the scope of a few verses, woes are pronounced, accusations are made and tempers fly. Amongst the many shortcomings of the doctors of the law high-lighted by the Lord there was one concerning the key of knowledge and the misuse of it. What is said about the key is capable of different shades of meaning but one aspect is clear, having taken upon themselves the acquisition of knowledge of the Scriptures as they then were, the lawyers neither conformed themselves to it nor did they ensure that others were rightly taught. The key was in the possession of a few. Responsibility to use it to open up the Word for the benefit of all lay heavily with them, but clearly this was not being done.

Christians generally are not readily given to boasting about achievements. Recognition as the fountain-head of wisdom and knowledge is not something that most would strive after. Nevertheless, through reading the Word and patiently waiting on the Lord, knowledge is acquired. Unlike the doctors of the law in the Saviour's day, there is for them no graduation ceremony, no diploma handed over when the course is completed, but day by day a good deposit is built up upon which the Holy Spirit can draw. The key to this, however, is in the believer's possession. Holding what is gleaned for personal satisfaction will not do. The key must be used to unlock the casket and release to mankind what has been designed by God for blessing here and in the hereafter.

*D*ay by day a good deposit
is built up upon which
the Holy Spirit can draw.

As for me and my house, we will serve the Lord. Joshua 24:15

A person's persuasion is nothing unless it is personal. It is valueless and empty if it is dwelling in the shadow of another's conviction. What someone else achieves for God cannot be borrowed to fulfil an obligation. Trying to duplicate or copy another servant's spiritual growth for the occasion will not do. Joshua's well-known and much quoted declaration, 'As for me' was not an echo of another's determination to serve God; it was his own exercise, and come what may he was determined to discharge it. Initial experiences with Christ in salvation were essentially individual. The singular aspect was all that mattered then and it is obvious that it was meant to continue that way until the end of the course.

Joshua's persuasion had its own compelling influence. Those of his household, whether family or servants, were of the same mind. To suggest that they were cowed or forced to take the same stance does an injustice to them and to a godly man. It must surely be that the three words, 'and my house' were the confident announcement that there was oneness of heart and mind. Everyone in Joshua's circle had the same persuasion, echoed in the words 'as for me', and they ranged themselves happily with the household's head.

Joshua and his house knew that there were great tasks to be done. They recognised the privilege of carrying the precious casket of testimony along life's pathway and to hand it over to others when their section of the road had been covered. There is still a bit to go. To be an onlooker or a participant is the question. The right answer is, 'as for me and my house, we will serve the Lord'.

*W*hen the children of Israel experienced the blessing of the sweetened water at Marah, the Lord revealed Himself to them as Jehovah Ropheca, 'I am Jehovah that healeth thee' (Ex15:26), hence the name, Jehovah Rophe, 'Jehovah heals'. It is the second of the compound names in the Old Testament, intimating the ability of the Lord to heal, to cure, not only in the physical realm, but in a spiritual and moral sense also.

Despite medical advances, disease is rife the world over. It is no respecter of persons, as it is said, 'it recognises no faces'. It is of course a witness to the fact that sin is rampant. Sorrow, pain and woe are ever-present and will be until the Sun of righteousness arises with healing in His wings (Mal 4:3). Until that day the world will struggle on, a little gained and much lost as the battle against sickness, disease and trouble continues.

Although the believers will be spared the horrors of the final chapter of man's history, the present has to be faced. If Jehovah Rophe was the great healer of the Old Testament, is that the end? Does He reach over into the next dispensation and continue with His healing ministry? He certainly did when the Lord was here. 'Go tell John,' He said, 'what things ye have seen and heard, how the lepers are cleansed, the deaf hear and the dead are raised, and to the poor the gospel is preached' (Lk 7:22). Surely today, behind what often appears to be heavens of brass, Jehovah Rophe is still there. Can He be relied upon to heal in His own way and in His own good time? Faith has no problem in answering the question.

Surely today, behind what often

appears to be heavens of brass,

Jehovah Rophe is still there.

'Cast thy bread
upon the waters and thou shalt
find it after many days.'

Cast thy bread upon the waters: for thou shalt find it *after many days*. ECCLESIASTES 11:1

Amongst the many challenging sayings credited to the wise man of the Old Testament, there is one which has always been in danger of becoming trite, and its meaning lost through its oft and loose quotation. It is Ecclesiastes 11:1, 'Cast thy bread upon the waters and thou shalt find it after many days'. This searching little verse falls naturally into three parts: casting, trusting, and waiting. Concerning the first, the sage did not say, and it is obvious that he did not mean, that the casting concerned something surplus to requirements. It was one's bread, the staff of life, the vital force supporting human existence. And, it should be noted, it was to the most unlikely place it was to be cast. Who would consider casting what was precious in the extreme upon such an unsteady platform? But then, things are not always what they appear to be in the ways of God.

The second challenge calls for faith. Said the preacher, 'thou shalt find it'. Having faced up to the challenge of casting, the second phase is trusting. Not the doubting which asks, 'Will it ever be found again?' It was cast upon the waters. It could have been carried hither and thither, never to be found or seen ever. But while it is true that God never fails or will ever be man's debtor, in the dire situations of life, things that normally are clear and positive, can assume shaky and distorted proportions.

The third challenge is the waiting. Once it has been decided to cast, that action is beyond recall. When finally reconciled to the uncertainty of the waters, that aspect is outwith human control. Possibly the third challenge is the most difficult to live with. The simple statement, 'after many days' is so indeterminate. But then, God's clock does not synchronise with the timepieces of earth. The preacher did not say, 'thou shalt find it soon', he said, 'after many days', and it is better to leave one's exercise with God, be it ever so costly, for who can say that 'after many days' will not, after all, be just soon enough.

SCRIPTURE INDEX